Are We Listening To Our Children?

Paolo Crepet was born into a serene, wealthy - and frequently happy - family in northeast Italy. He is a psychiatrist and sociologist, with a passion for art and music. Currently the professor of Youth Cultures & Languages at the University of Siena, Paolo has written more than fifteen scientific books, most of them about adolescent psychology. He has also written two story books. He is falling more in love every day with his little daughter, Maddalena, with whom he shares a beautiful red cat, Oreste.

Are We Listening To Our Children

Paolo Crepet

Bestseller in Europe

First published in Great Britain in 2002
by Piccadilly Press Ltd.,
5 Castle Road, London NW1 8PR

First edition published in Italy by Einaudi, 2001
Text copyright © 2001, 2002 by Paolo Crepet

A catalogue record for this book is available from
the British Library

ISBN: 1 85340 721 6 (trade paperback)

1 3 5 7 9 10 8 6 4 2

Translated by Patrick Creagh
Printed and bound in Great Britain by Bookmarque Ltd
Typeset by Textype Typesetters, Cambridge
Cover design by Fielding Design

Set in Palatino

Introduction

Bells that toll across the meadows
From the sombre spire
Toll for these unloving shadows
Love does not require.
All that I have my love; why longer
Bow to loss
With arms across?
Strike and you shall conquer.

'Underneath an Abject Willow'
W.H. Auden

If I were asked to write a letter to a baby girl about to be born, I would say this:

What have you heard so far about the world through the water and tight skin of your mother's belly? What have your barely formed ears told you about our fears? Will we succeed in wanting you without making claims, looking at you without filling your space with words, exhortations, prohibitions? Will we be aware of you even when you are silent, and respect your growing up without burdening it with anxieties and feelings of guilt? Will we manage to hug you without the physical contact being an agonising entreaty or emotional blackmail?

I would like your birthdays not to be laden with gifts – the sometimes shameless signs of our shortcomings – but full of attention. I would like the grown-ups you meet to be steadfast, consistent, authoritative: the qualities of the wisest. Consistency is what I would wish for you. And the awareness that in the world into which you are coming there are not only rules but relationships, and that both of these are equally necessary, two sides of the same coin.

I would like you to be taught to follow your emotions as kites follow the cheekiest, most wilful breezes; all your emotions, even those tinged with grief. I would like them to tell you that life also includes death. For grief is more than emptiness and loss; it brings something with it; it is positive as well as negative. Death is a witness that the best of us bequeath to others in the conviction that it will be of use to them. This gives birth to memory, the most beautiful memory of all, which is the story of our own identity.

I would like you to learn how to be alone: it could save your life. You must not resort to mediocrity to fill up voids, or beg a look or an hour of love.

Learn to create a life within your life and fill it with imagination.

Honour your uneasiness of mind as long as you have strength and can smile. Try to use it to inspire others, especially the timidest and most vulnerable. Give them the benefit of your courage, listen to their silence with curiosity, and respect even their worst fears.

It would please me if the person who comes to love you most can love your leaving, like a sailor who watches his old boat disappear beneath the horizon. And then you will carry that love with you for ever, concealed in your very heart.

Competition

Competition is everything

A lecture at a well-known ski resort. The weather is bad, the facilities are closed, so my audience includes a number of young locals. After the lecture they invite me to dinner. My table companions are mostly skiing instructors, congenial fellows, not at all sullen and tongue-tied as we city-dwellers usually imagine mountain folk to be. At the end of a long chat, one of them, particularly humorous and extroverted, advises me to visit the place more often, because in his opinion the family skiing holidays are the ideal times for anyone wanting to observe and analyse Italian families from the inside. I ask him to explain.

'I'll give you an example,' he says. 'All of us who work on the snow have made a rule for ourselves: never to accept children under the age of 4 in our classes. This is for obvious orthopedic reasons. Have you any idea how many parents lie about their off-spring's date of birth for the sole purpose of not allowing them to miss a single winter?'

Is this really true, or is the young instructor exaggerating? Next day the facilities at last reopen, and one only has to go anywhere near them to realise how right he is. Everywhere there are parents busy dressing up their infants (scarcely able to stand up on the snow) as if they were Olympic champions in miniature.

To convince me still further the young instructor advises me to be present on Saturday afternoon at the ritual closing of the week.

Any skiing holiday worthy of the name must naturally end with a competition on the snow, complete with starting-gates, stopwatches and tiny trophies for the tiny winners. A scanty crowd of adults and children has gathered near the hut at the top of the run, where the slalom begins. The children – all very small – are already lined up: skin-tight, bright-coloured outfits, helmets with designer goggles attached, their numbers prominent on their chests. One behind the other they wait their turn. Three, two, one . . . go! The stopwatches click into action, the children thrust with their sticks to get up speed, while on either side of the starting-gate the parents clap their hands and shout frantically. One of them – a 40-year-old particularly taken up by the event – yells at his daughter as she hurls herself on to the track: 'Bite that gate!'

In the evening, back at the hotel, I meet a group of parents still intoxicated with the achievements of their little champions. When I express my doubts, they reply with incredulity. 'Where on earth do you live?' asks one of the mothers. 'This is a competitive society, and the sooner my son learns that, the sooner he'll be able to stick up for himself and get on in life.'

But is it really as this lady says, all so obvious and taken for granted? Is this the only education we can, and want, and know how to offer our children? Competitiveness is, of course, a widely accepted part of our culture to be found in every corner of life; how many generations of children have watched talent quiz shows on television? What has a love of music got to do with a *Stars in Their Eyes*-style singing competition? Does no one think of the anxiety those children feel when they are called upon to perform in front of millions of television viewers, how much anguish they must feel at the idea of losing, of being rejected?

The ski instructor was perfectly right in saying that holidays are a good observation-post. I watched those parents, so arrogant and sure of themselves, always in a hurry, able only to give orders and make demands. If they are so restless, so incapable of putting aside a quiet hour for themselves or communicating other than by asserting themselves during a family vacation, just imagine what they might be like the week after, when they are thrown back into their stressful and daily routine.

But is it true that competition is the only possible technique for survival in this society of ours? Are the competitors, the winners, also the most untroubled and happy people? And must our schools be forced to fall in with the demands made by one section of our society, to transform all children into little managing directors? Or might they not attempt also to be peaceful places able to teach survival even to those children who do not wish to become gladiators but sensitive human beings instead?

Milan, a few months later. A meeting at the headquarters of the Lombard Association with young people in their last year of secondary school. We are speaking about their entry into the world of work. At a certain point, very late, the Chairman of the Association arrives for the customary pep-talk. He says common sense things, has the air of a benevolent father who knows all the secrets of life and thinks that all young people are slightly mentally deficient. During his brief address he says something apparently commonplace but actually highly significant: 'And then, dear boys and girls, get it into your heads that in life you need sharp teeth.' I tell myself that the great guru has arrived.

During the interval I ask a group of students what they think of the Chairman's statement. 'You see at once that that fellow knows how to live,' answers one of them, who seems to be their spokesperson. 'He's a winner, and we like winners.' 'How can you tell he's a winner?' I ask. 'You mean you haven't understood? Well, if you really want to be convinced, go right along to the end of the corridor and out on to the pavement. Parked on the left is a black Mercedes, and goodness knows how long it is. My father has a Fiat Panda. Between the two, who do you think is the winner? If winning needs sharp teeth, then we'll sharpen them every evening instead of brushing them with toothpaste. Right?'

Maybe those kids have their own good reasons for thinking this way. If we look around us without playing the simpleton, it is not hard to see that a considerable percentage of our children have grown up with this way of thinking and only seem to be impressed by adults who are competitive, a little cynical but sure of themselves, who firmly believe that life is either about success or nothing, and that all means are justified in achieving that end. In this view of things, not only the rules of ethics and morality, but also the necessary evaluation of merit simply get in the way. The achievement of one's aims is announced by flaunting the symbols that our community has apparently decided are the badges of success: power, money, ostentation, arrogance, violence. Is this the way many children would like their father or their mother, their guide in life, to be?

Every so often, during the debates in which I take part, someone gets up and gives us a good scolding, denouncing 'a society that has lost the basic values'. Often these are churchmen who, when May comes round and we pay our taxes, never fail to ask the tax-payer for the eight thousandths permitted by law to be given to the Church rather than the State: money, money, money, certainly not good works. So why should the children not avail themselves of these rules, make them their own with the same absolute assuredness with which their parents adopted them?

Many adults are convinced that this is the best of all possible worlds. Getting indignant about what is wrong seems to have become an anachronistic exercise.

If we look for it, a different and less submissive point of view may be found. We might begin to talk about a type of education based on other criteria, in which the emotions and affective relationships could act not as a limitation but as the catalyst of an individual's capabilities. Maybe our community could rediscover, for the generations to come, the joy and the pride of projecting a future less featureless and commonplace, less uniform and more creative.

Adult expectations

Are children mini-adults?

There is a programme that deserves to remain in the annals of the history of Italian television as the absolute rock-bottom from the pedagogical point of view: *Bravo bravissimo*. It is presented by that wizard of the cathode tube, Mike Buongiorno, and for various seasons has enjoyed great success. The protagonists are children dressed up and made to act like miniature grown-ups. They have to sing, play instruments, dance, and display their budding talents in the most serious and professional manner possible, worthy of an international competition.

As if in a gigantic medieval court, with children in the place of dwarfs, the adult public is entertained by the mini-champions of this programme. The spectacle is depressing, though I imagine that among the millions of regular viewers there are many parents who envy the fathers and mothers of those luckless children, and complain because their own little one refuses even to jump into a swimming pool.

You don't believe it? Then go and watch one of those Sunday morning football matches for children. You will see the touch-lines crowded with parents possessed by the devil and goading on their sons as if it were an Olympic final. If the coach dared to order *their* little champion off the field before full time they would eat him alive.

It may be that some adults think that school – and life in general – should teach people to stand out from infancy. Perhaps they believe that this would constitute some sort of guarantee. But being top-notch in the early days of one's life does not automatically lead to excelling later.

Salvatore Accardo, one of the greatest living violinists, explained this with reference to the Paganini Prize, the most prestigious of all contests for young violinists, and of more than thirty years' standing. It is held in Genoa, where selected young talents arrive from all over the world. They are professionals who have already embarked on outstanding careers. They have to perform a series of tests, all extremely demanding. At the end, three finalists are chosen, and from them the eventual winner, who is accorded the honour of playing Paganini's own violin, the legendary Guarnieri del Gesú preserved in Genoa's city hall. We could be forgiven for assuming that the final choice would fall on an artist of indisputable merit, destined shortly to become a great violinist. But this is not the case. Maestro Accardo maintained that of the more than thirty winners, only three have gone on to become truly great performers. This means that between possessing the ultimate in virtuosity and becoming truly 'great' there is a gulf that is not technically definable, but has to do with the young person's psychological make-up, his degree of self-confidence, his ability to cope with setbacks and deal with stress, his emotional resources . . . And these psychological features are certainly not maximised by a competitive upbringing. Quite the contrary.

Super-kids

Schools have acceded to the demands of many parents for unlimited results, just as many small children have adapted themselves to them. Families and schools have united to demand of our little ones nothing less than absolute perfection.

The children and adolescents who best match up to this insane demand are those who are 'top of the class'. They are the ones I call 'Abarth children', or the sons and daughters of the most unbridled ambition. Do you remember the small cars fashionable in the Sixties? To outward appearances they were normal Fiat 500s or 600s, but under the bonnet lurked absurdly souped-up engines that roared to impress the girls. They had one defect: they didn't last long.

Abarth children cannot be recognised from the outside, but their brains have been souped-up to make them go constantly at maximum revs. They not only have to achieve good results at school, they must shine at everything they do. They are the children who when they get home and tell Dad they got 8 out of 10 in Italian are asked, 'But didn't you always get 10? You're wasting time, not paying attention.'

The top-of-the-class children have no alternative, they live in one dimension: excellence. Many teachers share this absurd plot for the destruction of spontaneity to the point of having minted famous phrases such as: 'Your son is intelligent but could do better'. Which is the same as saying: 'Dear parents, you are right in forcing your children to work at top speed: go on and turn them into champions!' But if a child or adolescent is intelligent, isn't that enough? What more must he do? What, after all, is more important than intelligence?

With the exception of those few cases where a child has a natural talent and can do very well at school without much effort, being top of the class requires striving to a degree that exposes an individual to considerable psychological risk. Such children and adolescents cannot behave normally, they cannot make mistakes, they are thoughtlessly driven towards omnipotence.

They are usually not much loved, accepted only if they are brilliant, cherished only for their presumed perfection. The affection they receive is conditional, limited: 'I love you if you always get ten out of ten, otherwise I love you less . . .' Those parents, albeit unknowingly, are expressing lack of esteem. Abarth children are denied the basic right that every human being has from the moment of coming into this world, the right to its parents' love and unconditional acceptance by them.

The worst psychological damage does not result solely from being forced to excel at one's studies in order to be loved and accepted, but also from the gross error such parents commit in basing their overall evaluation of their children on how well they do at school. This way of thinking is founded on a tautology:

if a child does well at school it means it is first-rate, and this assessment is self-evident; if it does badly there can be no redeeming feature.

Now, apart from the fact that Italian schools are simply incapable of evaluating a child or adolescent as a whole person, how can we fail to realise that it is not right to force our children to be represented entirely by a school report?

We need only think of creativity. If schools do not know how to appraise it, parents run the risk of not appreciating it in their children, who in turn will consider it wholly marginal in their assessment of themselves.

Or consider the school-leaving examination. Is the school in a position to furnish an overall judgement of the candidate? If we ourselves had the right to sit for those 'maturity' exams, would the teachers be in a position to decide? Could we affirm that a candidate who has made a perfect translation from Greek or from English is by that criterion alone to be considered a mature person?

Sometimes the young Abarth seizes up, its souped-up engine conks out and the results can be very disruptive. This often happens at the end of a scholastic cycle: the youngster feels that he has lost the only ground on which he can gain the affection and respect of the grown-ups; he is scared of no longer existing. He tends therefore to hate and despise himself, to think he has failed. He goes so far as to have doubts about his circle of friends. Even his relations with the opposite sex are in danger of becoming uncertain, treacherous terrain.

Many of the roads that lead an adolescent to do himself harm in any of the countless ways possible start from an enforced perfection, from being driven to the very limit.

Parents, teachers, counsellors and the clergy all have a role and a responsibility: competitiveness is not for everyone, and above all does not pick out the best, only the least sensitive.

Precocious adolescence

A winter's night at Mestre, near Venice. The streets near the station are full of colourful figures. They saunter under the plane trees with scarcely a glance at the cars queueng up beside them. Headlights flash, tyres squeal. Suddenly a police car speeds into the forbidden market-place, scattering clients and voyeurs, picks on a small group of girls and follows them a little way. Two of them give in at once and are taken to the police station for checking. They are very young, it is the make-up that gives them a more mature appearance. They are sure to come from some East European country. The police examine their documents: no, they are Italian, in fact locals. They live in a city only a few kilometres away. They could be the policemen's daughters. One of them is barely 15, the other 16. They swear they made the choice of their own free will and that this is only the third time they have gone on the game. They told their mothers they were going to a disco. One of them says she found it amusing to see how many men were prepared to go with them for money. They insist they only did it for the money: at last they will be able to buy the designer dresses they have seen on some of their slightly better-off classmates. They will explain their purchases at home by saying they have been working as barmaids in a pub owned by friends.

What is shocking is not the facts of the case: women do not become prostitutes only because of dire poverty, but also when they want to treat themselves to luxuries without much effort. If anything, we are struck by their age, the fact that girls of 15 are making these choices is enough to give us the shudders.

Yet even this aspect of the matter is not so surprising. From recent research carried out by a group of American paediatricians it emerged that sexual development begins increasingly early, and that on average girls reach this stage at 9 or 10. This would appear to confirm the thesis – already widely accepted – that in our society the process of maturing is accelerating, to the detriment of childhood, and reducing the time for play. But this is only part of the picture.

Growing up is not a one-dimensional process. It has various components – cognitive, affective, relational, social – some of which have indeed speeded up in the last few decades. For example, the development of the cognitive occurs today under the impetus of the enormous wealth and variety of external stimuli provided by new technologies.

Some time ago I worked with a well-known theatre for children, the Teatro Testoni in Bologna. I remember that one morning a certain multimedia publisher gave the theatre around a dozen computers with keyboards specially designed for use by children and each equipped with an interactive CD-ROM. I tried playing on it, but it wasn't at all easy. According to the instructions on the box, the recommended age was 4 to 5 years. The usual sales hype, I thought.

Shortly afterwards a gang of children of just that age arrived. They kicked up a frightful din, and the teachers couldn't calm them down. Ushered into the computer room they sat on the coloured stools and started playing with the CD-ROMs. In a few minutes silence fell: eyes on the screen, hand on the mouse . . . It was as if they had always done it. They were totally absorbed.

If a child growing up forty years ago were put into an primary school today, the teacher would immediately send for a psychiatrist, thinking it had severe learning problems. In the space of a few decades the cognitive capacities of children have developed to a surprising extent, but this does not mean that our children are in all respects more mature.

In the same period of time, in fact, some other components of the maturing process have slowed down a lot. Consider social maturity, that is, the ability of a young person to take responsibility for himself and others.

Until a few decades ago many young men of only 18 had a family, a job, and a home of their own. Nowadays many parents lament the fact that their adolescent sons show little independence and great difficulty with respect to the rules of life. This reveals a notable degree of social immaturity (well described by the expression 'protracted adolescence').

One of the many reasons for this is the disappearance from children's lives of the places where they were able to play alone, without grown-up supervision. Courtyards, parks, patches of grass, these have all become inhospitable or dangerous, and parents forbid their children to play there. The children are therefore forced to spend their time in the constant presence of an adult, someone to take responsibility on their behalf for the rules of behaviour.

When I was young there was a day – maybe one of the most significant days of our lives – when mother said: 'Tomorrow you are going to school on your own.' This happened during the first years of primary school, and marked the official end of infancy. It was clear that from then on we would become more and more grown-up.

At one time, when young boys got together to play football, each had to agree to obey the rules of the game. Nowadays, children join sports clubs and delegate the enforcement of those same rules to an adult who acts as referee. They therefore grow up without learning to take responsibility.

Accelerated growth
and emotional autism

Sexual or emotional education

Another component of the maturing process in danger of slowing down considerably concerns the sphere of emotions and relationships. Emblematic of this is sexuality. If on the one hand biological growth, accelerated and improved by a richer, more balanced diet and better care of the body, has led to earlier sexual development (in the last three decades the average age for the onset of menstruation has fallen by two years), on the other hand this has not been accompanied by more satisfactory and rewarding relationships between adolescents. For this reason both school and the family should concentrate on emotional rather than sexual education.

The acceleration of some components of the maturing process and the inhibition of others causes a profound conflict of identity. Many of our children and adolescents find it hard to understand who they are, simply because on the one hand they have grown up increasingly talented, having been forced to learn concepts and technical know-how, exposed to the seductions of an adult world that for them is ever more virtual; while on the other they sense that the relentless pressure to grow up clashes with an awareness of the absolute impossiblity of achieving what they have been brought up to aim to do. In other words, it is as if we had taught 14-year-olds to drive but then refused to allow them to buy a car until they were forty.

Unnaturally accelerated growth leads to the development of increasingly complex expectations, which often conflict with an impoverished and disenchanted future.

Are we brave enough to take our foot off the accelerator? How, and by whom, will so many adolescents and young adults be paid back for their stolen childhood?

Teaching children how to take their time

A few months ago I was invited to a primary school in Rome which had a reputation for being open to new ideas in the field of education. As it turned out, I felt I had happened upon a small modern concentration camp in which the children begin their activites at eight-twenty and do not know when they will ever end. I listened to the animated discussion of a group of parents and teachers. They were wondering whether, between half-past four and six p.m., it was better for the children to dance, do gymnastics, or theatrical and musical animation.

Children are forced to 'work' nearly ten hours a day, like the workers of fifty years ago. They are whirled from one activity to another to show their parents and teachers that they know how to apply themselves to whatever is demanded of them, already trained to win a place in society – children worn out before supper time, incapable even of giving an account of what has happened in the course of a day spent like that of a business manager.

A child has a right to enjoy his free time not as a

nightmare but as fun and play and joy. Instead, not even days off are safe any more. Certain particularly sadistic adults have thought up an extraordinary stratagem to rout out those little sluggards who would like to spend their early childhood without doing anything productive. This invention is called 'entertainment', and the performer is usually dressed as a clown. The 'entertainer' is paid by the parents to turn a children's party into the umpteenth opportunity to reassure Mummy and Daddy of their offspring's gifts of communication and socialisation. Socialisation, what a blood-curdling word.

If the entertainer finds a child hiding behind the sofa eating crisps and drinking Coca-Cola, he at once upbraids him: 'Why aren't you playing with the others? Why aren't you getting in line for ring-a-ring-o-roses? Why don't you take part in the egg-and-spoon race? What are you doing there all on your own?'

Lack of socialisation has become the bugbear of parents and teachers. If a child tends to keep to itself they get worried at once, they consult psychologists and paediatric neuropsychiatrists. According to this bizarre way of thinking about childhood and adolescence, our offspring must be 'socialised' to average standard, otherwise they are not considered normal and doubts about their mental health take menacing shape in the minds of adults.

Many grown-ups refuse to understand that a wish to be alone is often a sign of maturity, so advanced as to make that child or adolescent feel how humdrum the lives of his contemporaries are. Development goes by trial and error, and the crises, the knotty problems of existence, are nothing other than phases in a growth process not foreseen or yet put to the test. To advance, it is sometimes necessary to draw back, just as an athlete does when he relaxes before making a great effort.

I tried to teach all this in several schools in Genoa, with the collaboration of a number of friends who were actors and musicians at the Teatro dell'Archivolto. The aim was to educate children to take their time, in other words to slow down, to listen not so much to others as to themselves. The children liked it a lot, the teachers less, the parents not at all.

This was not a question of encouraging children to be idle, as was claimed. Taking one's time does not mean squandering it but orchestrating it according to the dimension least familiar to children and adolescents, that of emotions and relationships. As a rule, in the rhythm of life that children learn, the emphasis is on the acquisition of knowledge; their day is a schedule of exercises, of rigid timetables. Everything has to run at hectic speed.

If we show them that the pace of everyday life can be less rigid and codified, more flexible and adaptable to the needs of each one of them, they will be able to see each period of time as having the potential to be filled with a new and unaccustomed dimension: the steady flow of their emotions.

It is not easy to explain to a child that one can take a minute rather than a few seconds to drink a glass of orange juice. The child will put up a certain resistance, not knowing what might happen during that suddenly expanded space of time; he thinks he will be censured for that strange and unexpected slowness. If on the other hand he learns to see that slowing up his thoughts and actions means enriching himself (for example, drinking more slowly will enable him to talk to his friends and laugh a lot more), then he will attempt to discover that different dimension.

To talk to children about time is important, because it has become such a rare and unexplored thing in our lives. The more of it we have at our disposal the less we know how to use it. We therefore have to teach them that taking their time signifies filling a space of restless confusion with meaning.

Children need to know that time is the home of communication, the channel of affection, the cross-roads of the emotions; that it is silence, looking, listening; that it is the kingdom of the senses, where touch, taste and manual skill once more bring a distracted existence into focus.

Time is curiosity about differences; it is imagining them and filling them with creativity; it is the secret passage of desires. But it is also solitude, sometimes even disenchantment.

If we succeed in giving our children the gift of time, we will teach them to search for it, to cherish it, and in this way, perhaps, they will be able to invent for themselves a life that is less of a foregone conclusion.

To understand how urgent this lesson is we need

only think of the possible side-effects (some of them already under our very noses) of the technological revolution now taking place.

I am not referring to the electronic economy, for even my mother used it unwittingly when she telephoned downstairs to the grocer to order a few slices of ham. Now, all over the world, purchases are made via the internet, but still by way of the telephone line.

The extraordinary and revolutionary aspect of what the technological networks will make possible has rather to do with time. For the very first time in human history one can earn the same or more by working less. Technology will help citizens of the western world (for many decades to come only we will be the privileged ones) to avoid bureaucracy, queues, meetings and so on. In a word we will save an enormous number of hours, and work will be concentrated solely on productive activity, liberating our creativity and imagination.

But here there is a problem: what will we do with the time stolen from work and from bureaucracy? Will we be capable of not working without feeling guilty? Since the world began, the culture of mankind has been based on work, on its ethics and rules. When we want to pay someone a compliment we say, 'He's a great worker!' If the internet is really going to free us from this torment (and anyway, mere survival is, for most of us, already assured by our economy), how will we use our time?

The decline of *Homo faber*

In a round-table discussion in Perugia I meet a well-known industrialist who, on hearing me make the above comments, begs me to desist: 'Please don't go on with these arguments, they make me nervous. It happens to me even when I see an advertisement for a Pacific island, with unspoilt beaches, a blue sea . . . I immediately start asking myself what I would do if I had to spend two weeks there without a mobile phone, secretaries, fax, email . . . I would die!'

The speaker is a very old man. He thinks like one of our Paleolithic ancestors, the only difference being that until a few decades ago we needed to work to live, whereas now work serves only to provide us with extras.

The future could therefore lead to the final decline of *Homo faber* or industrial man. The question remains – who will take his place? If it will no longer be work that defines us, what will give us our identity?

An old businessman friend of mine invites me to dinner in Verona. I meet some of his young colleagues, all busy earning a lot of money in the New Economy. I was expecting a boring evening talking about budgets and luxury cars, but there is nothing of the sort. For the first time in my life I spend an all-male dinner party talking about children! The explanation is simple. These rich young executives work hard for a concentrated period of time and then enjoy their wealth. How? Spending a lot of time with their children, for example. In other words, these men are for half the time 'great workers' and for the other half men of feeling; that is to say, they occupy their time with emotional relationships. They are men in transition to the future.

If we are going to work less, the remainder of our time will have to be employed in looking after our emotional lives; we will therefore have to slow down, to learn to listen to ourselves and know ourselves. This process is already largely under way; my grandfather allowed himself only a few hours of recreation on Sundays; I take the weekend off; I hope my daughter will have weekends of at least three days. But what will she do with the time when she is not working? Will she suffer deep anxiety like the industrialist in Perugia, or will she be able to live comfortably in that new dimension?

Perhaps in the not-too-distant future it will happen that when one man meets another for the first time he will no longer say, 'How d'you do? I'm an engineer', offering perfectly useless information about himself, but rather, 'How d'you do? I am at present deeply in love', liberating that element of his own identity – his feelings and emotions – which he has always undervalued.

For the children of today to become men and women 'of sentiment' tomorrow, it is essential that school should not aim solely at the establishment of an identity based on work, but also on non-work. Teachers ought to educate children to take their time happily and without any sense of guilt. Then at last our community will no longer judge its citizens only by their careers and how much money they make, but also by their capacity to form and sustain relationships, and their ability to nurture their emotions.

Virtual parents

The Italian Association of Separated Parents has suggested having recourse to the internet to 'maintain a continuous relationship with one's own child', and fill in the gap between one visit and the next.

The internet is an extraordinary resource and it would certainly not be a bad thing for a distant parent to speak to his child by means of a computer, provided with a web-cam, of course. And yet some uses of recent technological and scientific advances suggest a sense of surrender on the part of the community as a whole. Though possessing means of communication unthinkable a few decades ago, paradoxically we seem to have lost the ability to speak and listen, as if the meaning of our communication were lost for ever, replaced by chilly, virtual relationships.

Until fairly recently emigrants communicated with relatives left at home by telegrams or letters that took a long time to reach them; a video telephone enables us to see even the emotions written on a loved one's face. This progress can enrich our existence, but it threatens to distort the quality of our relationships.

We cannot, therefore, surrender ourselves to the idea that relationships with children – especially when they are fragile, as in the case of separated parents – can be replaced by a few sentences entrusted to virtual reality.

All the same, the fact that someone thought of this shows that the way we view our affections has become very arid. The suggestion from the Italian Association of Separated Parents shows that this is indeed how we now live, that our relationships are already 'wired', that we communicate more via mobile phones than through physical proximity. And all this has profoundly changed the meaning of our relationships.

None of this will come as any surprise to our children, growing up more with technologies than cuddles.

Some months ago, in a primary school in a big northern Italian city, the principal was forced to forbid his little pupils the use of mobile phones. At one secondary school a youngster proudly shows me his new mobile, tells me that it is the best, because it incorporates 'emotional icons', these being the symbols of the new communication channels for the emotions.

Virtual communication instead of hugs and kisses: what will become of a child growing like this?

Lessons for the senses

I once asked some children at a primary school in a Rome suburb to draw a cow and colour it in. Very few were able to get the shape right, and fewer still to colour the hide correctly. A couple of them were even convinced that it was violet, like the only cow they had ever seen in their lives – in a TV ad for a famous brand of chocolate.

If few children know what one looks like, still fewer know the smell of a cow, or have any idea of what it feels like to stroke its back. This problem is not confined to the young. In fact our daily lives are increasingly impoverished from a sensory point of view. The environment in which we spend most of our time is limited and limiting, and rarely does the use of the senses bring with it emotionally involving sensations. This is partly the inevitable effect of progress, for the struggle for survival of the human race no longer requires the strategic use of our innate faculties. Our abilities are measured by our cognitive talents: intelligence, memory, predictive or adaptive capacity, reactivity. We thus persuade ourselves that we are communicating better, whereas in reality we are only doing it more swiftly, and superficially at that. Not only the rituals of our emotional relations but also the game of love run the risk of being ever more degraded by this swiftness that relentlessly crushes the possibility of a more complete and varied understanding by way of the senses. Seduction is in danger of becoming a tasteless fast-food.

The emotional lives of adolescents have changed profoundly. Some of them describe sexual desire as a physiological need to be satisfied in as short a time as possible and with the least possible emotional and sensory involvement; like taking a bottle of Coca-Cola out of the fridge and drinking it in one gulp without even tasting it. We adults have evidently transformed our children, as Ingmar Bergman would say, into 'emotional illiterates', deprived of the senses like so many young autistics.

We have therefore to ask ourselves how we can reinvent a teaching method that will generate the ability to feel emotion, to involve the passions without fearing them as treacherous and dangerous territory. Emotional literacy can only start with the complete recovery of all our senses. School and the family must help children to regain possession of this enormous potential of theirs, all too often inhibited or removed altogether.

Children spend much of their free time watching television or videos, a means of communication capable, at best, of developing only two of the five senses: sight and (to a lesser degree) hearing. The video screen is not touched or tasted or smelled. Moreover, even sight and hearing are used passively. We therefore have to offer children more complex and invigorating teaching methods, proportionate to their increasingly high expectations.

By a stroke of luck a number of people are giving thought to this. The municipal Children's Museum in Florence and Children's City in Genoa show that intelligent action is possible.

Try asking your child if he has ever imagined seeing as a hawk does, or how a rattlesnake locates its prey in the dark, or how a crocodile sees under water. Taking children to such places as those in Florence and Genoa will help them to discover how absorbing it is to enter a world of the senses. Children are not interested exclusively in the Game Boy you gave them; they also enjoy learning to distinguish the smells of various animals or using their fingertips to guess by touch what the mysterious object is at the bottom of a box. The lesson might be useful to the parents too, for communicating with one's children does not mean only talking and listening, but also caressing, kissing, loving the smell and the taste of their skin.

Learning about pain

I often hear parents admit to not having been able to take their children to the funeral of a grandfather or grandmother for fear of frightening them.

If there is one thing that parents today seem to fear above all else it is talking to their own children about pain and death. Perhaps they do not feel up to it; perhaps they are too afraid of these two words because they reflect their own frailty. Pain and death must be expelled from the emotional life of a child because their meaning is disconcerting; they are at odds with the sugar coating we have spread on our children's lives, thus often rendering it cold and unreal.

Parents tell me that their children are afraid of pain and death. But what they are afraid of above all are our adult fears; their anxiety ends up by reflecting our inadequacy as educators, our discomfort and difficulty in coming to terms with suffering and loss.

Yet the experience of suffering and death is essential, strategic to the moulding of the identity of a child.

At one time, born into and growing up in far larger families than now, with several generations living together, it often happened that children witnessed the sickness and death of an elderly relative. In fact, such a dramatic event was (and still is) difficult to explain to a child, and therefore the parents and other grown-ups in the family unconsciously felt they had to adopt a strategy aimed at protecting the child from that grave and painful loss. So, in proportion to the seriousness of the event, the child received more cuddles, attention and acts of tenderness, and also departures from the rules of everyday life. For example, he was given something he had long been asking for but for one reason or another had not been given; he was allowed to play for an extra half-hour or given usually forbidden treats.

In other words, for a child the experience of death did not mean simply sorrow but also an increase of reassurance. So, grief and death did not appear to be only about loss, desertion and mourning, but also involved emotional compensation, a balancing-out in terms of affection.

Nowadays the situation appears to be completely the opposite. Children are deprived of these essential experiences to spare them any knowledge of pain and sorrow, a trauma considered useless. Thus, not only can they no longer witness and understand the sickness of their grandfather, but they do not even realise what his loss means to them. The denial of this experience renders the child more fragile because it has been deprived of the affection connected with sorrow and death. Not only will it not understand the meaning, but it can only fear and repress those events.

How does one explain a funeral to a child? How does one tell him about the people weeping, the coffin being lowered into the ground, about a person who will no longer be among us? At the funeral one does not speak to that child about his grandfather's death, but about his life: 'Do you remember when he used to take you to buy pastries on Sundays? When you went for country walks with his dogs?' Death can explain life. The child will also mature by thinking about that loss, those memories, those emotions.

On the other hand, what a child is frequently exposed to is the representation of pain and death, that is, their non-emotional and meaningless side. Thus real death is equated with the one seen hundreds of times in television films or on the news, but also in the even more virtual death in video games. What are present-day amusement arcades if not the consecration of death as a multimedia game? How many children and young people delight in killing monsters and Martians? For the new generations death could easily become a sort of 'Game Over'.

Pain should be restored to the teaching curriculum, a daily grammar lesson. The mums and the dads (but also the teachers and educationalists) should not be afraid of talking to their children about a sad event, should not teach them that they have to duck and avoid every setback life throws at them. It is important to get the odd bad mark at school, to face up to a disappointment in love, to be able to react when a wrong is suffered. In this way a child learns to know its own limits, to match up to disappointments, to come to terms with its own miraculous psychological mechanism.

Children are growing ever more precocious, so they very quickly assimilate the slightest hint of sickness and death. We adults have to adjust to this change in the process of growing up.

If we succeed, we will rear children who are less frail and open to threat, showing them that an adult is able to face the difficulties that crop up in life without being overwhelmed or annihilated by fear.

Some time ago I was invited to Foligno to present a book of poems written by the children in a secondary school in the city. Entitled *Small Stories of a Big Fear*, it was the result of some admirable work on the part of a number of teachers who had allowed their young pupils to dwell upon a recent earthquake and the devastation of their homes. An unending series of shocks had undermined not only their material well-being but also, and above all, the innermost stability of all concerned, day after day reducing their capacity to confront such unexpected and unnerving events.

That little book is absolute proof of the resources

children have at their disposal, far greater than adults usually credit them with. In this way a tragedy such as that terrible earthquake can become an opportunity for growth and maturity, an unforeseen and unforeseeable blow that shatters their enchanted world, a blow that first of all strikes and terrifies their parents, forcing them to reveal all their own frailty and inadequacy. In the eyes of the children only the old people are immune, especially the grandmothers, evidently moulded by still greater and more definitive misfortunes, and perhaps for this reason the only ones capable of being a point of reference.

Children find themselves almost forced to calm the fears of the grown-ups, and do it with enormous tact, managing to find the adventurous and exciting side even of a continuous battle against an invisible, insidious enemy who arrives by night with a rumble and a destructive force greater even than those imagined in the most frightening fairy-tales. Viewed in this way the earthquake becomes a fine story to tell other children who are luckier, but have not experienced a great emotional event. If a child has not had that experience, how do we explain to him the thrill of being saved by a great black knight who, scorning all dangers, reaches you with a ladder propped against your bedroom window-sill and saves your life? How do we explain that firemen are miraculous beings who come from the sky in the longest of nights, brave men who are especially fond of children and old people?

A catastrophe that becomes a resource, an enchantment that only a child can weave, the earthquake not only destroys and separates, but paradoxically succeeds in creating and bringing together. Fear unites people, forges stronger links than insipid everyday life ever can. And when such tragedies are remembered, the tone is appropriate to an event conducive not only to mourning and tears, but also to affection and tenderness.

This is the secret of every great fairy-tale. It has its monsters, terrors and sudden surprises; it reassures while it disconcerts. The greatest writers for children have been a mite sadistic, because they liked to scare their little readers, and yet none of them would ever have imagined that the wonderful stories they told would end up on a video cassette, and that a child would watch this sitting on a sofa on a lonely afternoon. The appeal of such stories takes for granted proximity, sensory communication, contact – not abandonment.

The children of Foligno teach us that fear, grief and loss also conceal an emotional side, and that life cannot be sanitised except at the cost of turning it into a banal television fiction; it is a single entity, inclusive of grief. Chiefly of importance to man are the emotions, which cannot be all sweetness and light.

For many people the outstanding TV event of recent years was not a football match, an Olympiad, or a meeting of world leaders, but the funeral of a young princess who died suddenly in the flower of her youth, and the death of a love story.

To feel that we exist, each one of us also seeks his own sense of tragedy.

Parents and
authoritarianism

The demands of the spirit

A glorious spring day. The hermitage is set among the vine-striped hills at Rovato, not far from Brescia. A handful of monks in a place of extraordinary beauty. On my way there I am expecting to give a talk to a few intimates, but instead the big hall and the long sunny loggia are crowded with young people. They sit in silence, looking attentive and curious. What brings them here? Certainly not the subject of the debate, let alone my name. It is the six monks who live in that monastery who draw those young men and women to that hilltop. They circulate amongst them, they know everyone and everyone knows them. The fascination must lie in their quiet, sober manner, an affability that never smacks of mere politeness, an erudition never flaunted but always consistent, a natural way of asking questions and listening to answers. In that atmosphere of great serenity one senses the conviction and tenacity behind the work of weaving bonds and relationships that has in turn created a common pathway, perhaps a shared language and culture, certainly a very strong feeling of belonging. One sees no mere forms and rituals in this place, but rather the gentle exercise of authority.

Last summer Rome was invaded by hundreds of thousands of young people from all over the world. Perhaps most of them came for reasons of faith, others just to be together and experience a great emotion, others again out of a desire to belong; and all of them to listen to the words of a Pope who is old and ill. They expressed the need for something not easily found nowadays, something our community does not express as often or in the way they would wish. Maybe those boys and girls were not even looking for a Pope, but simply for a papa, a father-figure, an authoritative adult able to dictate the rules, to make them respected and to respect them himself. Strangely enough, it cannot be easy for a young person in our times to find a mentor, to believe in a just cause, to have a hero.

A number of adults were probably perturbed by those thousands of young people. The world of the young seems to us increasingly contradictory. On the one hand their consciences seem totally free of the need for a myth and increasingly governed by opportunism and egocentric notions, and on the other they seem to hunger for spirituality and authenticity.

Yet the contradiction is only apparent. The cynicism and egotism we often find among adolescents are no more than a response to a frustrated quest. Authoritativeness is as important to growing up as rules are. And of the latter children have an absolute need; when they are not provided they ask for them, even at the risk of upsetting their parents.

What a mistake to confuse the just and proper need for authority with the useless exercise of authoritarianism! Not so many years ago a whole generation came into violent conflict with its own parents. In Italy this led to a transition which brought great conquests in terms of freedom (divorce, the closure of special schools and lunatic asylums). However, when that very same generation took on the responsibility of having children, it fatally confused the need to combat new forms of authoritarianism with the necessity of being authoritative. Hence arose an immense confusion of roles and relationships; mothers became their daughters' best friends, while fathers, rather than take a decision, preferred to absent themselves or say 'let it go'.

Thus, in a short time pugnacious, authoritarian parents were replaced by parents confused and lacking self-confidence, characteristics that aggravated the fragility of the new generations of children and adolescents.

Much has been said in recent years about the need for a parent to say 'no'. When they get to the point of saying to a child 'Do as you please', they have in effect given up on their authority. A 'yes' can in fact be a sign of indifference, and signify a lack of commitment.

Yet the most common method of bringing up children today is based more on 'yes' than on 'no', and this in large measure springs from the guilt that many parents feel weighs on them like lead, the sense of inadequacy in the face of their educational responsibilities, the fear of being too distant or absent or distracted, the knowledge of having left their children alone at home or in the care of a baby-sitter, the awareness of having made choices in life (such as the decision to live in a mononuclear family) too centred on the interests of the grown-ups. In addition, the parent or educator very often finds no means of diminishing his own guilt-feelings, which risk being magnified and weighing even more heavily on relations with the very young. Often it is fathers of the new generation who are most tolerant and inclined to agree to any request from their children. This is an (often unconscious) attempt to counterbalance a sense of guilt, which shows a sensitivity indubitably greater than that of their own fathers, but exposes them to a more painful sense of inadequacy.

There is no greater weakness in a parent than basing his own educative function on unresolved guilt-feelings.

How to say 'no'

Rules and prohibitions are important not only as ingredients of family and communal living, but also because they strengthen a bond. The answer 'no', if it is to be well received by a child, requires the presence of the parent or educator, so that it has an intrinsic relationship and therefore emotional value.

The 'no's', like good rules, are more of an aid to growing up than the 'yesses' just because they enable the educator to show authority.

A 'no', in order to have weight and value, has to be explained; it cannot simply be imposed. A 'no', like a rule, requires consistency, an essential component of authority. A father has no chance of being considered

OXFAM

VAT 348 4542 38

Volunteer here. Have fun.
meet new people & learn
new skills
Sign up in store or at
www.oxfam.org.uk/purchase

Mike T		SALES	F3851/POS1

WEDNESDAY 23 AUGUST 2023   11:19 347570

	GIFT AID 20100775603851	
1	C6 - LITERATURE	£1.49
	GIFT AID 20707616693851	
1	C4 - LEISURE/LIFESTYLE	£2.49
	GIFT AID 20704673733851	
1	C4 - LEISURE/LIFESTYLE	£2.49
	GIFT AID 20707203473851	
1	C13E. HUMANITIES	£2.99
	GIFT AID 20123606963851	
1	C14 - ACADEMIC GENERAL	£1.99
	GIFT AID 20430002473851	
1	C7 - CHILDRENS	£2.49
	GIFT AID 20430002473851	
1	C7 - CHILDRENS	£2.49

7 Items

TOTAL	**£16.43**
CREDIT CARD	£16.43

OXFAM SHOP: F3851
14 DUKE STREET
HENLEY-ON-THAMES - RG9 1UP
01491 577410
oxfam.org.uk/shop

Share your finds with
#FoundInOxfam

THANK YOU
Every item you buy or donate
helps beat poverty.

Donate to our charity shops.
Your unwanted items could fund work to
help communities overcome poverty.
Find out more here:
www.oxfam.org.uk/whattodonate

THANK YOU
Every item you buy or donate
helps beat poverty.

authoritative, and therefore respected, if, having bawled at his adolescent children that they can't stay out after midnight, the next day forgets his son's birthday and arrives at the party an hour late.

In the educational field the exercise of authority is all the more complex because it involves both parents. When a father makes a rule which is then contradicted or put in doubt by the mother, or vice versa, the educational credibility of both parents, and not just one or the other of them, comes a bad cropper in the eyes of the children.

The shift from authoritarianism to authoritativeness is a measure of the maturity of educational culture. Thirty years ago a number of German sociologists, referring to what had happened in their country with the rise of National Socialism, spoke of a 'fatherless society', meaning a community without rules, therefore non-emotional, incapable of educating in terms of relationships. Nazism was set up by 'autistic' adults, unable to feel emotions. Simone Weil wrote:

> *We live in an age in which most people feel confusedly, yet profoundly, that the culture of the Enlightenment, including science, provides insufficient spiritual nourishment, even if this feeling is about to lead humanity towards the worst of destinies.*

The need for spirituality implies and follows from the need for an ethical society, that is for a community of rules. Therefore the verb 'to educate' cannot be conjugated without the noun 'authoritativeness'. It is the dual concept that provides an emotional communion between parent/educators and children/pupils, and creates emotional 'belonging'.

Is it then possible that this happens only in a monastery or is it the work of some particularly brave parent or teacher? I recall a remarkable film, *The Dead Poet's Society*. What does that curious teacher of American literature offer his students if not a way of belonging achieved through the communication of a passion, or else an astonishing power of seduction? How can one teach the rules of a subject except by the exercise of gentle authority? In that film this necessity takes the form of a metaphor for survival. The boy whose father treacherously, one by one, denies him all his schemes for a possible emotional participation in something (the school magazine, the football team, the group of poet friends) is left with nothing but the realisation that life has lost all meaning. And he kills himself.

Indispensable to growing up is the feeling of belonging to something and someone; a loved one, an ideology, a flag, a faith, a friend, a master, a myth.

The young of a still vital world go on foot to see the Pope, others seek out the serenity of a monk, others yearn for a master capable of holding them spellbound, others again for a father who is not afraid of rules but imposes them with sensitivity.

All children and adolescents would like a 'Captain Courageous', able to lead them with strength and gentleness, giving of himself with competence and passion. Those who fail to find him will have no love and will grow up in greater isolation.

Carrots and sticks

What a strange country it is in which the citizens make a vast collection of money to raise the fortunes of the 'Blue Telephone' (the Italian equivalent of ChildLine) and then, only a few weeks later, the Court rules that striking a child with a whip should not be considered maltreatment, but merely 'an abuse of the means of correction'.

In the school I went to there was a mistaken sense of order and of rules. I belong to a generation in which the teachers beat the children on their hands and made them stand behind the blackboard for hours. It is with horror and sorrow that I remember my primary school teacher who made me kneel for an hour on a handful of peanuts (in those days we all wore shorts) because, according to her, I had behaved badly. Nor can I forget the comments of the teachers at my secondary school when they saw the welts of a belting on the skin of one of my classmates. 'What can he have done?' they asked one another under their breath. As much as to say that a father had a right to beat his son and that no teacher was authorised to interfere in the home life of his pupils.

No educationalist has ever been able to convince me that this was a sound educational approach. Even the old rule based on rewards and punishments seems sophisticated in comparison with those harsh correctional methods.

I might be asked whether a smack should be considered an abuse or downright maltreatment. A slap can escape from even the mildest parent, but in any case it sadly betrays our inability to understand and educate. It is like thinking that hitting a radio will make it work better.

Setting a value on slaps and blows implicitly means reasserting a male role in the upbringing of children. The father figure has often been capable of demanding but rarely of giving. The father asks to be respected as head of the family but then absconds, both physically and emotionally. For this reason authoritarian upbringing has always suited the male, simply because it can be exercised without him having to be there. All it needs is for him to come home late, give a wallop to the son who deserves a reprimand, and stretch out on the sofa to watch TV, convinced he has behaved like a responsible, strict father.

When I meet someone in a marital crisis, I often hear: 'We're not separating for the children's sake; if it had been left to me I'd have done it at once.' This is emblematic of the modern version of adult-centred upbringing. The point of view of children or adolescents is always the last to be considered. It never even crosses the mind of that parent that it is not right to subject a child to the day-by-day transformation of a loving relationship into indifference, if not into hatred. If a parent really wants to do something for his children, he should listen to them. He would then learn that they don't want hypocrisy, they detest that make-believe of pretending to be a united family just because it is Christmas Eve or Grandma is coming to supper.

In this way such a parent teaches his child that personal pride is not that important in life, and that self-respect is not good strategy.

Loving others and loving oneself

Take a look at a family in a restaurant on a public holiday; there are the parents, the children and perhaps a grandparent. Note how the parents behave towards their children, how they talk, their tone of voice. You will see that if a child is present the tone will probably be shrill, communication will be almost always one-way, from the person giving orders to the one who has to obey them. Try to count the reproaches. They will certainly outnumber the praises, even in the simplest things such as peeling an apple. Do you see? The child holds the fruit in one hand and the knife in the other; his movements are clumsy, inexpert, and he gives an anxious glance at one of his parents. Wait a few minutes and you will see either father or mother impatiently snatch the knife from his hand and say: 'Give it to me and I'll peel it for you, otherwise you'll cut yourself.'

Such is often the first lesson in lack of self-esteem. It

is a long process, and sometimes lasts a lifetime. I remember a man of about 50 who, after many ups and downs, had left his wife and children and, having no alternative, had gone back to live with his parents. His mother, then nearly 80, after a few days of getting used to the new domestic arrangements, had resumed the tones and contents of a discourse interrupted thirty years earlier: 'Are you going out? It's cold out there, are you warmly dressed? Be careful, walk slowly, it's raining . . .'

Behind many kinds of anxiety we find the difficulty a parent has in trusting his or her own child. That in turn often masks an absolute self-assurance: 'If it weren't for me, heaven knows what would become of you.'

This egoism answers to a need: that of sustaining a role (parenthood in short) which would otherwise be destined for a natural decline.

Cesenatico, a resort on the Adriatic. A meeting with parents and teachers. We talk about young people and the Saturday night road deaths, tragically frequent in these parts. In the front row are two women who at first talk among themselves in low voices, but then increasingly loudly: 'Tell the professor what you did about your daughter . . . tell him about the camper.' My curiosity aroused, I ask the lady dragged into it by her friend to explain.

And this is what she says: 'I have a 16-year-old daughter who, like all her friends, has for some time been begging to be allowed to go and dance at the disco on Saturday evenings. To start with we put the matter off, delaying our decision, but finally we had to give in. The first weekends were terrible. I couldn't sleep until the girl came home, and as Saturday approached the atmosphere in the family was unbearable. A solution had to be found; we could neither be worried to death nor force her not to see her friends. And so I thought of my husband's camper . . .'

The idea is brilliant. About midnight on Saturday the mother fetches the camper, the daughter (dressed for the disco) clambers aboard and off they go. They park, the girl joins her friends while the mother puts on her nightgown and slips into bed with a good book until she nods off. At dawn the girl knocks at the door of the camper, mother wakes up, and home they go happy and contented. Ingenious, eh?

Apparently yes. I ask the woman: 'How long will this go on? There will come a day when you can't take your daughter to the disco in the camper, and how will you spend that night? Will you trust her? Will she have become independent and responsible, and therefore capable of self-esteem?

Self-esteem, self-regard, these are signs that a person has reached a level of independence, and knows he can rely on his own resources. Perhaps that mother was thinking more of her own anxieties than about her daughter's growing up.

Teaching an adolescent self-esteem is indispensable, indeed it ought to become a strategic, educational principle right from primary school. Our educational method ought to be founded on the promotion of independence, whereas all too often it is based on the depersonalisation of the pupil by rewarding the lowest levels of cognitive ability: 'Understood?' 'Yes.' 'Then say it back to me.' Our system of learning tends to be founded not on strengthening the individual and therefore the independent resources of the learner, but on proving the abilities of the teacher.

Learning to be independent

I remember having learned this simple principle many years ago while working at a university in the city of Aarhus in Denmark. A colleague invited me to visit a primary school situated near my department. The syllabus was disconcertingly simple. Everything, it seemed, revolved around the most important event of the day: lunch. The children chose which of their number would that day make out the shopping-list, collect the money, go to the nearby market and buy the necessaries. Then, those who had been to the market had to account for what they had bought and hand it over to the children assigned to the cooking. Finally they made lunch and everyone ate together, teachers included. In this way the children not only learned reading, writing and arithmetic – indeed they learned it better and more quickly, being stimulated by activity that concerned and interested them directly – but above all they learned to be self-sufficient, to get by on their own without needing a grown-up there to supervise them. That school taught children self-respect. When they grew up they would develop their independence and strive to achieve it as a strategic part of their lives.

Love is the most sublime – and sublimated – form of self-esteem. Love is a project, a challenge, readiness to believe. But to believe in one's own future one has to respect oneself.

To love is therefore to love oneself. There are, unfortunately, mothers and fathers who teach children not to love. How many times have I heard young people say that the worst mistake their parents ever made was getting married? This implies feeling unwanted, living one's life as the product of a misunderstanding. An adolescent has a right to grow up without feeling as if he is made of glass, looked right through by those who ought to love him – empty, superfluous ectoplasm, a non-person.

John F. Kennedy said that the hottest places in hell ought to be reserved for those who, faced with our moments of painful transition, stayed neutral. To love, and to love oneself, means combating neutrality or indifference.

Junior racists

Can children be racists? Thirty years ago this question would have seemed purely rhetorical. Our country had faced the problem of racial coexistence in a very limited and casual manner. A child today meets a child of another race in every school or park.

It is important to concern ourselves with their reactions, because we know these will determine the future of coexistence in our community. It is a question of either triggering conflicts or constructing a social culture in which different ethnic groups can live harmoniously together.

Until a few years ago, Italy enjoyed the benefit of a positive approach to civic issues, as if we were fully equipped, spiritually and culturally, to live with racial differences. But the experience of areas in which the racial mix had actually proliferated without too much discord was a delusion. It was thought that the Catholic tradition had laid the foundations of peaceful coexistence, based on tolerance of differences (though I distrust the word 'tolerance' because it implies a feeling of superiority in the one doing the tolerating). We were convinced that a modern country would have produced enough strong antibodies to wipe out any ancient, barbaric forms of intolerance at birth. It did not happen that way. Recent anathemas pronounced not only by political leaders but even by certain cardinals oblige us to review our hopes and illusions.

To be convinced that children have in part absorbed this recent and widespread feeling of racial distrust we need only read the results of the social research carried out in the last few years, based partly on the written work of many pupils in primary and secondary schools. But not even these enquiries have answered the basic question of whether an attitude of fear and repulsion towards what is different is innate, or caused by the imitation of such behaviour in the family or social environment.

The great Moroccan writer Tahar Ben Jelloun gives a clear answer. He maintains that racists are made, not born, and that everything depends on how one is brought up and by whom. He states:

> *The spontaneous nature of children is not racist. A child is not born racist. And unless his parents or his family have put racist ideas into his head, there is no reason why he should become so.*

Ben Jelloun's point of view is idealistic, weak with respect to the cultural identity of a child and misleading regarding the duties of adults. There is no such thing as the spontaneous nature of a child that is not produced by the influence of and adaptation to the environment in which it lives. From the moment it opens its eyes the external world conditions its certainties and fears. Certainty is what it sees around it, fear is the idea that all this might disappear. It is very unlikely that a child is born and grows up in a perfectly multi-ethnic environment. Rather than being a cultural question, this is a problem of identity, which a child centres upon that of its own parents and the social nucleus that it grows up in. It wants and desires what the adults desire, and fears what they fear.

The 'spontaneous nature' of a child is therefore neither racist nor anti-racist; he does not make judgements, but expresses emotions. For a child differences of skin, behaviour, ways of being, never take on an ethical or moral significance, and for this to happen they have to be taught it.

If, therefore, we can agree with Ben Jelloun that a child is not born racist, what this writer omits is equally obvious: that it does not come into this world anti-racist either. It is certainly not by preserving a spontaneous nature that we will grow up as a generation less afraid of diversity. And if adults communicate fear of what is different, how can we fail to foresee that children too will become frightened of the 'other'?

Children do not learn only from long, laborious lessons, but also from apparently banal remarks and acts: an insulting remark from Dad heard at a football match, Mum's gesture of irritation towards someone who asks to clean your windscreen at a red light. These are drops that fall one by one into the soul of a child, increasing his distrust of those who have a different-coloured skin or do not share his religion. Thus, in silence, a little racist comes into being.

We are sometimes unaware that the profoundest type of racism is not directed against people who are different and alien to us, but against those we ought to love the most. One of the least manifest but most widespread forms of racism is called paedophobia.

Crimes against children

Paedophilia and paedophobia

A couple of years ago I was visited by a young couple who lived in a city in southern Italy. He ran a small business, she was a housewife. Their tragedy was written on their faces: their two children, aged 10 and 12, had several times been seriously molested by an uncle living in the same building. This had been going on for many months, and the uncle had blackmailed the children into silence. Finally the mother, struck by the sudden behavioural change in the younger one, managed to get the whole story out of them. The parents wanted to denounce the uncle, but were afraid of even worse repercussions on the children. I tried to tell them about the bureaucratic delays of the law and the need to protect the children from the intrusions that the various stages of a trial might entail.

A few weeks later I learnt that with great courage these parents had denounced the uncle and had faced the courts, the indifference of many people and the sarcasm of the violator himself.

For months I heard nothing more, until they rang up to tell me that the uncle had been acquitted.

They revisited my consulting room. They could not understand how their children could have been subjected to another form of abuse, this time legalised. They told me of the countless hours they had spent being interrogated by magistrates, experts, psychologists, social workers. And then the threatening telephone calls, the fears of every kind, the anguish of a family fighting alone to protect the dignity and integrity of its own children. And finally the snub of the acquittal, the mockery of relatives and neighbours, the uncle free to meet his victims daily and to smirk at them.

No one wanted to believe those children.

Adults scarcely ever believe children. Our community is always ready to give priority to the rights of adults rather than those of children. Protecting children is difficult even for those whose duty it is to do so.

In these last few months the editorial offices of the newspapers have been full of blood-curdling news items about children exploited, tortured and killed, the travels of 'respectable' gentlemen who frequent the most repulsive sex markets, stories of rapes and molestations going on with the complicity of the family, professional men who spend the night buying children via the internet. Horrifying facts appear to induce not only contempt but barely concealed morbidity: the most popular television news programme, at peak viewing time, transmits photographs of violated children as casually as items about the economic situation.

Paedophilia stands out as one of the most disquieting phenomena, not only on account of its exceptional ambiguity, but above all because it seems to us the most odious act of violence, being as it is directed against the defenceless. Playing upon their innocence, the paedophile, in the most degraded way possible, represents the quintessence of hatred towards children, while the hypocritical censure of not a few adults masks a sordid, ill-concealed complicity.

In the midst of this unspeakable inconsistency there emerges in all its brutality not only the instinct of many adults to override the wishes of the very young, but also an inability to purge themselves of the more deep-seated evil: paedophobia.

Paedophobia is the cult of contempt for the weakest, indifference to them, inability to see their point of view. It is forcing a child, already the victim of violence by an adult, to suffer that of the bureaucratic machinery of the law, unending interrogations by magistrates and experts. Paedophobia is suggesting (as many of my colleagues have done) the application of one of the many manuals that parents should follow to save their children's lives from the dangers of paedophilia, rules which if strictly adhered to would force our children to live in constant anxiety and terror of anyone who came anywhere near them.

Paedophilia is not a poisonous mushroom, an anomaly that our community is on the point of simply rooting out; it is born of and nourished by a phenomenon far more widespread and disconcerting. The odious complicity that enables the paedophile to spin his slimy web mirrors the most loathsome obstacle that social progress has not managed to overcome. It may seem strange and paradoxical but this community of ours does not succeed in loving children, just as it distrusts young people.

Isabella Bossi Fedrigotti writes in a newspaper comment on the umpteenth horrifying crime committed against a child:

> *In our decorous and more or less privileged life . . .*
> *we did not imagine that there were people, thousands*
> *of people, prosperous and respected adults who enjoy,*
> *who take pleasure in seeing children tortured and*
> *killed.*

This lady probably lives on another planet. These crimes are not only committed in slums, but also in the damasked drawing-rooms frequented by the cream of our society. We cannot pretend we are living in a world sustained only by healthy principles: how many mothers and fathers, even if rich and powerful, abandon their own children, hit them every day or force them to witness scenes of incredible physical and psychological violence? How can we fail to see that there is a connection between insensitivity and bullying, and that the latter could not exist without that particular absence of love?

Can we deny the evidence that many paedophiles were themselves violated as children? And how can we fail to see that such brutalities can become time-bombs primed to burst, even years later, into acts of contempt or aggression towards oneself or others, until they reach the most extreme and hair-raising forms.

The many ingenuous souls who make up society would like to make children believe in a fairy-tale world divided between the good (privileged) and the depraved, who are aliens born and bred on another planet and who land in our world to be cruel to children and contaminate our irreproachable morality. This is a Manichean view that divides the reponsibility between damaged DNA and irrational impulse or *raptus* (a magic word used by journalists when they don't know how to explain a crime), which cause an irreproachable person to unpredictably go off the rails.

A paedophile is not born but made, and the spores of this horrendous plant are sometimes hidden in the 'normal abnormality' of the emotional relationships of many families.

Powers of persuasion

In the beginning there was *Carosello*, the half-hour television programme of advertisements that came on at supper-time and delighted children and grown-ups alike.

With the proliferation of commercial television channels, the assault on children as an ideal vehicle for the conquest of new areas of the market has become ever more insistent; children have become not only important consumers of snacks, satchels and video games, but they also influence what adults buy. Words and brand names seen on TV are stored in their memories, to be fished out when they go with Mum to the supermarket.

If the very young are therefore a strategic target for an increasingly large number of marketing professionals, we run the risk of being remote-controlled to buy the things that most impress our children. One of the major London advertising agents, Saatchi & Saatchi, long ago set up a department to produce television ads that would appeal directly to children and adolescents.

The consequences are not hard to imagine. Advertising does not promise a greater freedom of choice but a restriction, a reduction. Let us try to multiply the seductive effect of advertising on children and adolescents in terms of widely consumed goods. The risk is that their tastes and preferences are dictated by others, meaning that they will buy only certain things and they will all buy the same things: they will grow into a stereotype, just as some television programmes risk influencing people to adopt standard ways of behaviour and cultural tendencies.

This situation cannot be prevented by stupid censorship, which is unlikely to succeed in any case, but by the assumption on the part of the adults of greater responsibility for educating children. Otherwise the mass media will have things all their own way.

Is it therefore right for parents and educators to be increasingly worried about the influence television may continue to have on children and adolescents?

Grown-ups often use television as a scapegoat in any issue concerning young people, from rocks hurled on to cars on the motorway to hooligans in sports stadiums, from its obsession with sects or extraterrestials to anorexia. It appears that the young can do or think nothing except what reaches them through the cathode tube.

It is not that television is blameless, but to claim that all children and adolescents are slaves to the box is going a bit far.

The influence of television

With what is shown on television there is a tendency to overestimate the content and underestimate the environmental context in which it is seen. Let us take the example of a child who sees a monster in a cartoon and then can't get to sleep or wets the bed. Is this caused purely by the contents of the cartoon? Not exactly, because out of a hundred children who watch the same cartoon very few will show signs of distress. What changes things and makes a difference is the subjectivity of that particular child and the context in which it has watched the cartoon. It is obvious that if the child was alone and had to wait some hours before being able to express his fear to a parent, the emotional 'fall-out' will be quite different to that of another child who watched the programme close to someone who at once calmed his fears with a joke or a hug.

This argument does not apply only to the relationship between television and children, but with adolescents as well. Think of anorexia. We all know that this serious condition is in part influenced by examples encountered through the mass media. But the problem is not only linked to the influence of television; we must also consider how our way of life has changed, quite separate from that influence. It is likely today that the anorexic prototype of Kate Moss coincides with a profound crisis of the family structure that is no longer able to oppose and cope with the tribulations of adolescence.

If we were really convinced that children's behaviour, especially when violent, is produced by what they see every day on television, it would be enough to make us turn the thing off permanently!

On the other hand it is years since any research has been done in Italy to shed light on the negative effects of television on young people. Our homes have been flooded with the most violent cartoons without anyone turning a hair. But this does not allow us to think that a television programme can act as the direct cause of particular types of behaviour; at most it can influence those already so predisposed.

During a debate in Milan a woman tells me: 'My 5-year-old daughter wakes up an hour before she needs to, switches on the TV and watches the cartoons. How can I stop her?' Plainly I don't have to tell her that the set is equipped with a switch; the problem is that those cartoons fulfil the convenient role of baby-sitter and the parents are unwilling to give this up.

I have no wish to absolve television and deny its responsibilities, but nor can I ignore those of the parents. If we try to avoid them we run the risk of hitting the less important target. In the last five years in Europe young people between 15 and 20 have shown a marked lack of interest in the TV screen in favour of video games and the internet. Today we blame television, tomorrow it will be the virtual networks. It is an endless denial of responsibilities that certainly does not help us to understand more about children and adolescents.

The French psychoanalyst Bernard Bensaid once told me a story. On his way home one night, a man meets another searching for something under a street lamp. 'Can I help you?' he asks. 'Thank you, I've lost my house keys,' replies the other man. So the pair of them start searching. After a while the first man, having found nothing, asks: 'Are you really sure you lost them here?' To which the other replies: 'Not really, it's just that here there's some light to see by.'

Some forms of malaise stand in relation to television as those keys did to the street lamp; it lights up what is nearest and most consoling to us, but it distances the truth. The real reasons lie elsewhere, not far from our hearts and minds. It is neither television nor the internet that make for distress in children and adolescents, so much as the unwillingness of adults to be there for them.

Italian school system

Who is school for?

To assess the state of Italian schooling is a complex matter, and it is no use making facile, generalised accusations. Even so, certain facts are clear. Out of 1000 children enrolled in the intermediate school, only 173 go on to get a degree; out of 10 who obtain the middle school certificate, only 6 graduate from the secondary school; only 42% of 25- to 30-year-olds possess a diploma (as opposed to 90% in Germany, 80% in Great Britain and 60% in France); in industrial and commercial technical institutes 60% of the students fail to average a pass mark. We need only analyse the most recent data on qualitative standards to discover that the position of Italian schooling is even more unimpressive compared with that of our European partners. If our primary schools can bear comparison with the other countries of Europe (Italy is seventh out of fifteen countries analysed), in middle school we notice a deterioration (we are eleventh out of seventeen), while with secondary schools we drop to the bottom of the list.

The worst of it is that a similar survey carried out twenty years ago showed an identical picture. Not only, therefore, is the situation bad but it shows no signs of getting any better.

The rebellion of the majority of Italian school-teachers against any possible evaluation of their teaching abilities threatens to create further rigidity in a system which is already one of the worst in Europe. Everyone knows that getting a degree in a subject does not mean knowing how to teach it, but it is difficult to find a parent willing to rebel against the fact that his child's teachers draw a salary without anyone being able to check up on their teaching abilities. Why on earth should we place our children in the hands of an incompetent? On the other hand, why should a good, up-to-date teacher not be rewarded, even with a bonus?

A commission of experts recently nominated by the Ministry of Education suggested a change in the initial training of teachers, including a year of apprenticeship with pupils. Even in this matter, much fierce criticism was heard from certain influential trade unions.

Maybe there is still no wish to acknowledge that school should not give priority to the rights of the teachers, but to those of the children and adolescents.

Just after the war there came to Italy, in point of fact to Rimini, a disciple of Piaget, the pioneer of infant psychology. She was convinced that Italy would rise again from destruction and hatred if it believed in its children. She set about raising funds to build a kindergarten that was run according to the teachings of the master. A few elderly citizens of Rimini still remember that lady going round the building site to make sure the windows were sixty centimetres from the ground. And when she was asked to account for that eccentricity, she replied: 'Why do you want your children to have to stand on tiptoe to see if it's snowing outside? Let the teacher bend down!'

School

No school year starts without the usual disheartening news, depressing statistics, politicians interviewed about reforms never carried out, strikes and labour disputes ritually announced. Mediation with a teaching body that is often dissatisfied and demotivated gives us a glimpse of what has not been done or has not ever been attempted. The Italian school system veers between concrete hopes of change and serious dangers of regression, prey to a strange contradiction: everyone – teachers, pupils, parents, educationalists – has good reasons for criticising it, but nothing seems to shake it out of deep-seated resistance to change.

Yet something has changed, and it would be unjust not to mention a few notable developments in the right direction. We need only think of day nurseries and nursery schools. Nevertheless, our judgement must also be measured against our greater expectations with regard to educative processes. As citizens we have at last begun to demand a bit more for young people, and perhaps the cultural means now more available enable us to discuss matters with headmasters and teachers without the feeling of being underdogs, which until a few years ago characterised our relationships with school.

Today there is discontent with the overall quality of the education provided. And if macroscopic data depict some progress in the teaching field, it is nonetheless true that over 5% of pupils abandon their studies without gaining the middle school diploma, compared with the late 1980s when the rate was almost 10%. But this improvement is partly due to less selection in compulsory school, where the percentage of failures is constantly dropping (from 12.6% in 1985 to 6.9% in the last school year).

Dissatisfaction arises above all from the feeling that our schools are not altogether adequate for the requirements of present-day society. We have not yet succeeded in making them places for the young, in which the allocation of time and the subject-matter to be taught and learnt are richer and more flexible. All too many schools are not yet living spaces devoted to the well-being and interests of children; they do not provide them with a place in which to express themselves, to form lasting relationships and learn from them, to compare experiences and emotions in a sort of permanent laboratory, protected and guided by the knowledge of the grown-ups to whom they are entrusted.

A new pact

We have to negotiate a pact between families and school in which each takes on new competences and obligations. Our community has undergone a profound transformation that has touched every corner of our lives, and there is an urgent need for family and school to adapt to the effects which this transformation has brought with it.

School must be reinvented. We need to begin with the time set aside for education: only full-time (which is the rule in all industrialised countries) is capable of meeting the needs of young people whose families have become so small. The parents work all day, and the grandparents are for many reasons almost always unavailable.

Given that children and adolescents will spend the greater part of the day at school, the family must devote sufficient time on weekends, evenings and holidays to its own educational responsibilities, to become aware of itself as a family.

Why then are these changes unwelcome? Why do teachers' associations rebel against the prospect of a revision of school hours? When it comes to having no school on Saturdays, why do many parents protest that this will prevent them from carrying on with their own jobs? In Sweden or the UK, where most children do not go to school on Saturday, do parents have no professional interests or activities to safeguard?

The problem of school hours is by no means secondary. Full-time would enable school to pass from mere instruction to education, offering time, place and activities aimed at providing not only knowledge, but above all opportunities for growth; it would enable the family to be aware of each other at times not limited to bits and bobs of meals or Sunday football matches. It would at last be a self-sufficient school, where children begin and end their commitments without having them absurdly prolonged by hours of home-work.

A different way of organising time devoted to living and working would enable us to see things from the point of view of the young.

The muddle with regard to schooling exists also on other levels. Think for example of the daunting Russian roulette that parents have to go through at the start of every school year. 'Let's hope my daughter can be enrolled in 2C and not 2A. That would be a disaster!' If a bad teacher can have such an effect on the cultural, formative and moral future of our children, how can we allow this to depend on an absolutely unpredictable factor? Why is it that, among teachers, training, teaching ability and even the time devoted to their professional duties can vary so enormously?

Teachers and children

Playing a role in psychological and cultural development

Despite the obvious limitations of the present situation, many teachers, for various reasons, find themselves playing an important role in the cultural and psychological development of their pupils, and are increasingly getting involved in their problems. They are adults against whom the children measure themselves daily; they represent strategic points of reference for them while they are growing up. Teachers ought to be models of consistency, tolerance, willingness to listen and ability to judge. A lack of authority among sometimes negligent parents means a lack of figures of authority to whom the young can refer, and this in turn leads to loneliness and insecurity. Just as they have their friends, they would also like to find teachers with whom to identify. At such delicate moments parents and teachers ought to know how to collaborate, and not confront each other in a mean-minded game of roles and power.

But it is also true that school often becomes a convenient scapegoat for the evils of our society, even to the extent of handing to teachers the entire responsibility for everything that concerns the young. We need to analyse the variables of a complex situation, establishing school as a strategic and indispensable institution for the reform of the whole community.

The young are dropping out of school more and more because they find it increasingly difficult to see it as relevant to their lives and culture. In the classroom they too often feel they are not listened to but only judged, and this undermines their relationships with the teachers. We therefore need to start again, to re-establish the quality and dignity of the vocation of teaching.

The school we want

In failing to forge strong links with both students and teachers, school holds no appeal. Everyone regards it as alien, as if it does not matter to citizens or the school staff, or even to the government. The impossibility of enjoying school is a measure of the impossibility of feeling a part of it. In the last few years many teachers have left the profession banging the door behind them, without having any real discussion, or even explaining their reasons for leaving.

This at least partly explains their often indignant reaction to criticism not expressed aggressively, but in the hope of finding an opening for understanding, an impartial interpretation of things, based on the analysis of facts and not the clash of prejudices.

Every time I meet teachers in public debates or refresher courses I come up against the same obstacle. I find myself criticising schools to the most sensible and least submissive members of the profession, in other words, the wrong people. If I talk about the inefficiency of a school, I am not referring to the teachers who keep up to date and buy books at their own expense. The problem is the others, the less scrupulous teachers. How many of them do nothing but teach, without a second job? The question of full-time school is fundamental. It is not a matter of punishing teachers, but of asserting the dignity of teaching itself, as a task that must not only be done, but be seen to be done (therefore not done at home), fully recognised and remunerated and must include extra training. It seems odd to me that teachers accept payment for what no one can check up on: the work they do at home. It is like a Fiat worker taking a windscreen wiper home with him to be fixed.

And what kind of training should there be? Are teachers in a position to recognise and deal with their pupils' worries, and is it their responsibility? Are they paid for this? Perhaps they could learn if they taught in a school that was ready to shoulder those worries collectively, instead of delegating them to the duty psychologist. If it claims to educate, school is obliged to listen. And listening is a real problem with teachers.

A young mathematics teacher I meet during a refresher course in Bologna tells me about a particularly depressed and sullen pupil of hers. She asks him what is wrong. The child talks, the teacher listens. A few days earlier, just before closing time, his parents' little jeweller's shop had been robbed. Two well-dressed young men entered the shop. Neither wore a mask. One of them suddenly drew a pistol, while the other, with a knife, pinned down his mother in the back room of the shop. Much of the jewellery was the property of the wholesalers, so only partly covered by insurance.

The teacher suggests that he might talk about it in class, if only to get it off his chest. This inevitably gives rise to a lively and sometimes violent discussion. 'If I were in your shoes and met those thieves I'd kill them!' 'What we need is more police.' 'No, that's not right, we have to stick up for ourselves.' 'The police are no good, they're all corrupt.' 'What we need is the death penalty . . .'

The teacher tries to explain how complicated the problem is, but it's no use. The other children gang up on the boy, accuse him of weakness. Angry words fly, echoing what grown-ups have said. What frightens the teacher is not the violence of what they are saying, but the fact that she feels useless, distant, unable to communicate. How is she to stand up to this violence, how can she affirm her own right not to think that way without risking losing her authority?

But what that teacher did is in fact the highest form of rapport. By allowing the children to express their own opinions as best they can she reverses the role of the teacher; rather than confining herself to supervising and judging, she allows the children (and allows herself) space and time to listen to the grief and trouble of a pupil. In so doing she helps him to escape from the confines of his anxiety and confers dignity on anger and reason on helplessness. She acts in such a way that the young people are able to come to grips not with some abstract topic but with the very real problems of one of their schoolmates. All in all the subject of the confrontation is less important than the method. In this way one gives meaning to teaching, bringing children up to live their lives. The fear young people feel grows apace if they are afraid of being left alone, of not being protected by adults. Giving vent to their feelings brings this fear to the surface, to be worked out in due course. Parents are often confused and this leads them to fail to make a distinction between things and people, to neglect to teach their children that the latter are always and in every way the most important.

When teachers explain their own ideas they cannot expect to be understood right away. Persuasion requires tenacity, and time. Let us make it possible for young people to come round gradually to value our strength and consistency, supposing we have them; in this way, without being aware of it, they will learn to use the highest form of communication.

But there can be a thousand opportunities for relationships in a school equipped to grasp the possibilities of doubt and meditation in all the stimuli that culture urges upon us. The expression of complex things has to be a slow process, and a teacher's skill rests in making the pupils see it as something they have discovered themselves, not as a truth handed down from on high. All too often syllabuses that have to be followed leave no space for reflection and understanding.

The impact of theatre

Take for example theatre, but a special kind of theatre. To know a little more about it we have to go to Medicina, a small town near Bologna. Every year in late spring it is the setting for an event that might appear marginal but is in fact an intensely useful experience for many parents and teachers. The performance (co-ordinated by the Teatro Testoni of Bologna) is called 'Worksong' (*Canto di lavoro*) and takes place in the middle of a field. The boys and girls who take part in it share a passion for the theatre: they are fascinated by the use of words, of gestures, of the body. They give their contemporaries the performance they have been working on throughout the school year, but more important still, among themselves and with the actors who have assisted and supervised them, they talk about the meaning of their love of theatre and their wish to communicate it.

Theatrical performance is an extraordinary mise-en-scène that gives the young a chance to take a new look at themselves, their own conflicts, dramas and fantasies. There is a particular atmosphere about it, a feeling of gathering in a certain place to meet others and lay one's own life open. Those who have taken part in this enterprise have things to tell that go far beyond the set and the wish to perform: they create bonds far stronger than are usual in the daily lives of adolescents. This is what those youngsters are looking for, a chance to communicate outside the prescibed rules and spaces, an opportunity to listen to others quite free from conventionalities and commonplace rituals.

Working together — among themselves and with grown-ups — they succeed in finding the right way of saying what no one has ever wanted to hear, what others have only touched on. There they spew out their anger, give vent to it, act it out. And that anger fills with feeling, produces meanings, influences even those who wanted to reject it. Contemporaries who didn't want to understand, or who didn't manage to do so because their words found no common ground, inevitably find themselves involved and lose all their bashfulness. Theatre sheds light on darkness, overcomes the stupor of embarrassment.

Take a girl who hasn't eaten or had her period for months. Which is more useful to her, an hour of Italian literature or a situation in which the language of her tormented body is at last free to express itself? Take a hyperactive, violent boy. Which will do him more good, a course in cybernetics or a chance to exploit his own exuberance in order to make himself the centre of attention without being instantly excluded? Both things together, probably, but then why does school provide only the literature and the cybernetics?

I do not, of course, regard theatre as just one more assignment, but as a free and creative choice, in which the text is the cultural world of the young — what they have to tell us.

Naturally there is a certain risk, and this is well known to the wonderful, sensitive professionals who have given of their time to enable these young people to create a physical and mental terrain completely new to them. The risk is that this experience induces new and greater expectations on the part of grown-ups. Indeed it changes not only the participants, but the school that promotes it. As one schoolmaster said: 'Now that we have lived this experience together it's impossible to go back to being a teacher as before.'

Who stole the dream?

Chiaravalle is a small commune just outside Ancona. It has an abbey, a tobacco factory and a few other industrial plants, and also a newly restored theatre and a reception centre for young people. There is a great wish to be up and doing in these parts. The kids have painted the walls of this centre, and several other walls besides. Farther on, along a tree-lined avenue, gigantic letters spell out the message: 'Defend the lime-trees, paint the nuns'.

A few days later I am in Lucca to meet teachers who, together with their classes, are taking part in the project called 'Imagining the City'. We ask the children what they would like in their neighbourhoods, what is lacking in the city. The answers are many and various, but one request receives unanimous support: 'Why don't you build us a wooden house up in a tree?' The idea is put forward again during a meeting with the mayor and he, having considered the question, asks me in an undertone: 'In your view, what will the health authorities say?'

Are our children and adolescents free to dream? Is there anyone willing to pay attention to their creativity?

A town in the Marche a few months after the terrible earthquake. A group of teachers asks me to help devise a way for the children to come to terms with their fear. We decide to get them to write, draw and paint, and they fill pages in their notebooks and write beautiful poems. In the end it is the children themselves who want this work to be preserved, so a printer is found and a book is printed. At its formal presentation, one fine May morning, the Town Hall is crowded, the children excited, the teachers proud. The most interesting stories and the best poems, as judged by the children themselves, are then read aloud. Each child reads his own work, and is awarded a prize by the mayor. All except one: Mirko, prizewinner for not one but three poems. But Mirko is not there, he doesn't read his poems, he doesn't get his prize.

This worries me, and I ask the teachers about him. They reassure me that his home was not damaged, he is not ill; he is simply going to be flunked. Because Mirko doesn't study, he is very bad at maths and English, he disrupts the lessons and often plays truant.

And yet he was the budding young poet of the town: so his classmates had decided. His poems were the most beautiful of all.

I am not laying a charge of insensitivity against the

teachers in that earthquake-stricken town. They did a great deal for those frightened children. What happened to Mirko is a metaphor of our educational culture. The absence of that little boy contains a double implication, that is to say a denial and a promotion. Twenty-seven or twenty-eight children were denied Mirko, in other words an emotional resource, with his poems and his talent. At the same time all those children, except him, were promoted on the basis of their mediocrity, a bare pass-mark in maths or English. What will Mirko think when he comes to school to do the whole year over again? 'You can't cheat me with poetry any more . . . I'll get six out of ten in every subject and just you see if they don't pass me.'

Every year, those children, and thousands like them are not only deprived of imagination and creativity, but they are taught that such a dream leads to failure. Better to opt for a tolerable mediocrity and no emotion, just as so many grown-ups have done.

School cannot afford to lose Mirko, children cannot grow up without dreams and hopes, without utopias. Our whole community would lose its chance of self-renewal, of self-reflection. Mediocrity reduces everything to the same level, makes everyone the same. Imagination and dreams shine the spotlight on our inner resources, the secret well-spring of our being.

Boredom, creativity and happiness

The curse of boredom

As on every Saturday evening, a girl goes with her fiancé to watch the cars racing madly round a roundabout near Bologna. One night there is a sudden flash, a car goes off the road, mows her down at 20 years old.

The case causes a sensation, the press and television describe it in gruesome detail. The Mayor and the Prefect of Police issue fiery statements exhorting the forces of law and order to exercise greater control; they decide to send a patrol to keep an eye on that traffic circle for a night or two. But there are dozens of other roundabouts surrounding that city, and no doubt most other cities. Once the clamour and the shouting dies down, the whole affair is swallowed up in silence, no one wonders any more what became of the thousands of young spectators of clandestine car races. Were they scared off by the words of the Mayor? Did they melt into the night when a police car drew up alongside?

Every year hundreds of young people are killed after a night at the disco or at the pub. Each time this happens the authorities flex their muscles, plan a big strike, then for a few days there is talk of closing the night-spots earlier . . . then summer arrives and the profitable business of entertaining the young elbows conscience aside.

Nor is it long since the nights when teenage boys took to throwing rocks on to the motorways from bridges. Then too the arguments and soul-searching lasted as long as the television news. Then there were explanations, hypocritical comments about generations 'no longer able to tell right from wrong . . . who no longer know what values are'. And when the puppet show of collective sorrow comes to an end, what happens? Can our community really grasp what the behaviour of those young delinquents really means? Can it understand that they are merely metaphors, that is, warning signs that potentially concern thousands of their contemporaries?

A few weeks after those events I meet a group of pupils at a school in Valenza Po, near Tortona, the scene of a tragedy (in which one young woman was killed). I ask them what happened after that terrible night, whether in some way their daily life has been affected by the event. No, nothing. Nothing happened. The same bars, the same pubs, the same Saturday evenings racing through the mist to reach some disco to spend all night at. The same boredom. In their eyes I see the surrender of those who don't expect much from life, and I wonder what has kept them from going on hurling rocks, and what will be the next game of dicing with death.

And the grown-ups who beat their chests in despair, who wept over the tragic fate of the young, what did they manage to do? Nothing. Or rather, they put up signs under the bridges over the motorway.

'Do you suffer from boredom? How much does it affect your daily lives?' I ask the secondary school pupils of a city in Umbria. Result: about two-thirds of them declare that they get bored every day. For a teenager it is not enough to live in a prosperous, beautiful city built on a human scale, where everyone goes around on bicycles, where the environment is respected and there is full employment.

Boredom is a real threat in the life of an adolescent. Boredom is the feeling that has given rise to countless calamities great and small in young people of every generation; it underlies the most diverse forms of psychological stress. True boredom comes from inside, not from outside factors. The most irreparably bored are often the privileged youngsters, the ones who already 'have everything', including time on their hands that never seems to end and they don't know how to use. A child left to wander at will through an enormous toyshop, when the marvel and frenzy of the first impact is over, does not know what to do. The very excess of stimuli discourages creativity, and makes the child passive and apathetic.

Boredom is a kind of frustrated expectation, and the expectations of the young are higher in proportion to the standard of living of a society. Imagine asking your grandmother what, at the age of 18, she would have liked to do when she grew up, and then ask her what in fact she thought she would do. You will find that there is not a great difference between the two answers. Now put the two questions to an 18-year-old today, and between the first and second answer you will note an enormous gap, and that gap indicates a frustration, a difficulty in forging one's own identity and objective in life.

Boredom is something learned. One can easily teach it to an adolescent by protecting him from everything, showering him with luxuries, depriving him of volition, imagination, the need to experience new things. He will grow up without knowing what a wonderful and important thing it is to create things for oneself, to be enterprising and daring. Anyone subjected to such a rotten training tends to become resigned and compliant. He is brought up to fear ambition because it entails sacrifice, to live life passively, always expecting the most from others. He gets used to living by making claims on them.

If, therefore, it is possible to learn to be bored, it must be equally possible to teach children not to be bored when they become adolescents and grown-ups. The only antidote to boredom is creative intelligence. It is by no means easy to come by, but let us try asking a parent how many times he has taken his son or daughter to a museum or has spent half an hour (not two minutes) with them watching the sun go down. Few parents think it is more important than signing the child up at a swimming pool or a sports club.

Try asking an adolescent to describe how his father behaves when he comes home in the evening. He will paint a picture that has been the same for decades. The same gestures, the same sounds. Repetition kills all the best feelings. Creativity is akin to the strongest emotions, which have to be re-invented day after day, certainly not taken for granted.

How many young talents vanish, swallowed up by a school system likely to squash individuality? How often do we admire the sensitivity revealed in a drawing by a child of 5 or 6 years old, the freedom of form, the ability to put colours together in an unusual way? Three or four years are often enough to persuade that child to draw a house with a smoking chimney and a path leading up to the door, exactly like the other children, all equally condemned to the same mediocrity.

All too often schools do not help parents to believe that intelligence must be a free expression of the individuality of their children.

'Your son is intelligent but he doesn't apply himself.' This has been trotted out for years by generations of teachers. So saying they imply that in our educational culture intelligence and the ability to express oneself must be viewed in terms of application, the exercise of cognitive abilities on a lower level: all children do sums by memorising the multiplication tables, but this does not prove that they are intelligent. Such abilities in fact have nothing to do with the need and the willingness of a child or adolescent to feel that someone is keeping an eye on his learning process. A teacher capable of supervising and supporting an individual project, the development of the expressive ability peculiar to each pupil or adolescent, will never feel reassured by the progressive erosion of the uniqueness of their pupils. Perhaps such a teacher would say, or at least think: 'Your son is intelligent, *therefore* he does not apply himself'.

Boredom and lack of creative intelligence do not

need orthopedic surgery, but action that will revolutionise how each child and adolescent learns.

If instead of thinking up palliatives that insult the intelligence of those at whom they are aimed – sending police patrols to the roundabouts, closing the discos an hour earlier, putting notices on the bridges over the motorways – we began to reflect on the motives which lead a young person to spend time in a degraded and degrading way, we might even devise a new era in policies regarding the young. To understand what a teenage boy or girl is looking for on Saturday night we must try to see what they do not manage to find during the week. If from Monday to Friday their time passes in flat monotony, or is felt to do so, it is obvious that on Saturday they will seek out something special, exciting, unusual. A young person (but also a grown-up) has a right to live his own emotional life to the full.

So then, instead of devoting ourselves to checking the weekend excesses of our young, why do we not attempt to render their everyday life less dull?

I am not thinking only in terms of one family or one school, but of a whole community capable of gratifying its own young people.

Months ago I had the pleasure of meeting the Mayor of Forlì, a very well-informed and accessible person. We talked about a possible project for a vast area of public property, now disused, though in the very centre of town. My suggestion was to use the space to set up a centre devoted to the creativity of the young. A place open day and night, in which to put on shows of all kinds, to equip a music recording studio, to paint, to read their own poetry aloud, to eat in restaurants run by themselves. In a word, a workshop for youthful imagination, the projects of the young, their cultural output. But also a place where they can simply be, can meet each other, pass the time together. Not a question of finding an alternative to the discos, but of offering a response to their right to do something exciting without waiting for Saturday and without having to depend on beer, pills, and speeding through the fog. Is this possible? Is it a utopia? Why can a city not supply an answer to the needs of its own younger citizens? Why should a mayor not aspire to combat their boredom and stimulate their creativity by establishing a centre that would also enable many parents and teachers to gain a less superficial understanding of the young, to accompany them at a distance in their process of growing up without being afraid of them?

From Forlì I await replies, and above all, the young of that city await them. Confidently, of course.

The shifting sands of happiness and passion

Invited to a meeting by the committee representing the pupils who have taken action and 'occupied' a secondary school in Rome, I find an interesting atmosphere, much excitement, much more creativity than in an 'unoccupied' school. After the debate one of the girls asks me to read a questionnaire drawn up by her and a group of friends and submitted to their schoolmates. The questions have to do with their lives, expectations, hopes, plans and so on. Glancing through the pages of that inventory I note that there is one word that never appears: happiness. I ask the girl to explain this. They too have realised as much, she says, but they find that word 'embarrassing'.

Does this embarrassment conceal a premature fear of living? Our culture finds it hard to come to terms with happiness, and mostly it is adults who are embarrassed to talk about it to the young. We are still hampered by an atavistic fear of the precariousness inherent in the lives of our ancestors. Centuries of Christian abstemiousness have taught us to experience pleasures as if we should be afraid of them, and resign ourselves to the aim of mere survival. For Sigmund Freud, 'the price of the progress of civilization has been paid for with a growing reduction in happiness due to an increasing sense of guilt . . . mankind has always clumsily bartered happiness for security'.

That made sense for our grandparents' generation, who lived without ever knowing whether the war just over would be the last war (or epidemic or famine) of their lives. Today the majority of the citizens of this small corner of the planet stuffed with excess can consider themselves sufficiently secure, but even so they are unwilling to speak about happiness.

To paraphrase Theodor Adorno, we should agree that

happiness is like normality: we don't *have* it, it's inside us. No one who is happy can know he is, for to see happiness – Adorno would say – we have to step outside it. For this very reason previous generations have found it hard to suggest really positive methods of education, and we therefore still prefer 'doing' to 'feeling'. Thus for an adolescent it has become difficult to cope with the most natural question a grown-up ought to ask: are you happy? One psychoanalyst, editor of a well-known letter column in a newspaper, tells me he is surprised that no one ever asks him if he feels happy.

At one time people suffered because they had nothing, except poverty, hunger and death. Now, having acquired everything we need, we have preferred accumulation (of money, objects, possessions: our very identity?) to communication and feeling. We have pretended not to know that the true quest for happiness is through authenticity and moderation. Aspiration to happiness implies great demands, the experience of real emotions. What if many young people are afraid of these?

A girl in a secondary school in Mantua confides in me that of her many fears the greatest is that of falling in love. 'What a swindle!' I say. 'What do you do about it?' 'Well, I've found a solution: I like the boys I don't like all that much. The moment I feel that one of them might make me lose my head, I run for it.'

This is what many parents and teachers have transmitted to their children and pupils: that great emotions are dangerous, they are quicksands where it is perilous to venture. Better to aim for mediocrity, to cling to the banality of a regular income, better a plump tax return than a lofty spirit disquieted and disquieting. Many grown-ups prefer to dampen the ardour of the young.

Education seems increasingly cut off from feelings.

At Pordenone I have a meeting with the parents and teachers of primary school children. To the teachers present I suggest a simple test. I ask them, as they walk next day between the rows of benches, to stroke the head of one of the children suddenly and for no reason. Eight times out of ten the child will leap out of its seat. A caress seems to have become a prize, or exceptional gesture rather than an obvious and perfectly natural form of emotional communication. 'And just as well!' declares one woman in peremptory tones. 'I send my daughter to school to be taught, not stroked!'

I tell a group of teachers in a primary school in Verona about the outburst of rage I heard from one mother: her 7-year-old son with learning difficulties had had his special support teacher changed eight times in one school year. What could be more cruel than this? One of the teachers present tells me candidly that in her school the headmaster has a theory about detachment, holding (and she says agrees) that bonds of affection are prejudicial to learning.

Two women teaching in a school in Treviso show me a confidential letter received from their headmaster, in which he calls upon the teaching body to abstain from any physical show of affection so as to avoid misunderstandings, given the deep concern of many parents after so many cases of paedophilia reported in the press.

Of the mother in Pordenone, the teacher in Verona, the headmaster in Treviso, I ask what they understand by teaching. How does one educate without a relationship; how can one establish such a connection with a child if no provision is made for emotional communication, and therefore a hug or a kiss?

A literature teacher in a secondary school in Grosseto asks me, 'How can I teach about emotions?' 'By teaching Italian with passion,' is my reply. 'I lost all my passion for it twenty years ago,' she says, not even seeming that upset about it. Are we to believe that many teachers in our schools no longer know what passion is? That many children and adolescents who have not been shown or been brought up to feel emotions will be able to seek them and exhibit them as adults? Isn't this the very antithesis of good teaching?

The photographer Oliviero Toscani once taught me a game. Give a dozen 9- to 10-year-olds everything they need to colour with. Then give each a sheet of paper bearing a large square subdivided into lots of little squares. Ask the children to colour in those spaces as they think fit and to sign their names on the sheets. Collect all these up and get the children distracted by other games, so that they forget about what they have just done. When enough time has passed, give each child another sheet identical to the first; but before you tell them to colour it ask them to keep absolutely quiet, to close their eyes and concentrate hard, then to think of the person they hate most at the moment. When it is certain that they are thinking intensely about that horrible person, tell them to open their eyes and colour in the squares at once. Then compare each child's sheet with his previous one, and which is the better? The second one every time: the hate-sheet. Not on account of hatred itself, of course, but because between the two performances they have felt an emotion.

To stir someone's emotions is to transform their abilities; with children and adolescents it helps to bring their powers of expression to the surface. Every educational project ought to bear this simple principle in mind.

Fear of the unknown

Giulia, who lives in a big city in the north of Italy, spends every winter weekend at a well-known ski resort where they have opened a near-vertical ski run on which the craziest speeds can be attained. She is an intelligent, good-looking, comfortably-off girl, and it is really difficult to understand why she is so determined to risk her neck every Sunday in an insane ski race. When interviewed, she replies: 'In those few seconds I feel myself sucked down into a wonderful whirlpool, I know nothing else ... for a moment life and the outside world no longer exist.'

Giulia belongs to a generation in which many have learned to live on a tightrope. They walk without thinking of the world around them; they are aware of the chasm beneath their feet and feel it as a real, intense thrill.

For these young people emotion is the square metre on which they are standing; there is no reality outside what they can touch. Many of them have lost the dimension of travel; they do not seem interested in using their imagination, nor do they seem to feel the need for any real escape. It is paradoxical that they, who more than any previous generation enjoy the money and ability to get about, show such a marked resistence to the idea of setting out, as if they had been frozen to the spot by the fear of getting lost. Perhaps prosperity, instead of working as a catalyst, acts as an emotional blackmail that ties them down.

Those frequent comings and goings to and from distant and different places belong in the past: how many young people of either sex still hitch their way round the world? Now they spend a night in Rimini or go to the United States to study for a while, with their return ticket booked. The young of today prefer a safely planned journey to random travel, taking things as they come. This difficulty in feeling themselves citizens of the world can be inferred from one typical aspect of the writing they produce: it is often based on their own experience or self-centred, limited to the tiny world in which they live, and also incapable of speaking to more than one generation.

Leonardo Sciascia wrote: 'The pleasure of travel is that of knowing, in the places one goes to, either nobody at all or very few people; of not having letters of recommendation to deliver and appointments to meet; of not having commitments towards oneself; to see without fluster the things that we wanted to see, which are usually not all that many . . .'

Perhaps it is this search for the unknown that many of today's generation direct inwards, confining their curiosity to virtual reality. For these young acrobats, who live on the wire strung above the roofs of our houses, recklessness is not crossing mountains or deserts or journeying to east or west, but what they can create at home, in their own nests.

These young boys and girls want to imagine the world rather than know it. Perhaps what they have glimpsed of it, namely the part of it we reflect back to them, must be alien to them, and ugly with it.

Parenting with love

Banishing guilt with a present

A well-known professional man comes to talk to me about his 16-year-old son with whom he has a very bad relationship. The two of them have not spoken for months, the son does worse and worse at school, the family atmosphere has become explosive. I ask him to go into more detail, to tell me about some episode that particularly disturbed him, and he picks on a small daily event that has aroused his curiosity. For some weeks, first thing in the morning, the son picks up his father's mobile telephone and types the same three words into the phone: 'Dad remember moped'. This man, who has a thick white beard, also recalls that some evenings earlier, while stretched out on the sofa watching television, he had the feeling that someone had stroked his beard. Turning quickly, he saw his son standing near the sofa.

I ask him how long it is since his son last gave him a hug. Years, he says.

I do not think it takes a psychoanalyst to realise that the boy wanted to leave another message on that telephone, for example: 'Dad remember me' or 'Dad let me touch you'. Is it easier to ask for a moped or a kiss? And how long does it take to buy a moped, and how long to kiss or be kissed when it hasn't happened for years?

The ritual of giving is complex. At times one does it spontaneously, at other times a gift masks a kind of blackmail in which the gift doesn't come free, but always requires something in return.

Different languages meet in this ritual, those of giving and asking, of bestowing and receiving. All too often an object becomes the simplest solution, answering an unconscious need to balance up a relationship that is seen to have become one-sided.

This should be well known to any educator. If a teacher could visit the bedroom of one of her small pupils she would understand a lot; for example, by counting the objects piled on the table and the bed. If there are lots of them, too many, then something is wrong. Too many teddy bears and dolls signify a plea for forgiveness on the part of the parents: forgiveness for being absent, or too seldom available, or distracted. Presents can easily become pawns which grown-ups have to swap in order to assuage their own guilt feelings.

If a parent were to pluck up courage and, instead of buying an object, were to simply be available, he would understand that a request for a present is often nothing other than a request for affection. Gifts are often bestowed just because they don't require much of the giver, merely some money.

If young people grow up seeing all their requests side-stepped by the gift of an object, they will tend to idolise objects at the expense of relationships. Indeed, they might fear the latter to the point of wishing to avoid them. We might therefore make a gift of something else, the availability of our time, for example – a small gift capable of producing an enormous emotion.

In our culture the language of giving runs the risk

of being reduced to an exchange, to a bartering of objects and reassurances. Objects replace feeling and intuition, sensitivity and an acceptance of our differences, leading to uniformity and monotony. Any intercourse that might otherwise have passed between the generations is thus lost, and like crazy mortals we and our children lose the power of speech, understanding, agreement. All affection is lost in the terrifying simplification of existential silences, broken only by the chink of money. Thus any possible richness in diversity vanishes. Nothing is left but a mechanical exchange, a reflection of the gulf that separates us.

It becomes impossible to understand anxieties, feelings of rebellion, obscure language used to express the unswayable. No one will ever again understand the diversity of the other, his sorrows, his fears and his longing for affection. All that is left in the end is loneliness, gift-wrapped and tied with a silver ribbon.

Alone on the *Titanic*

Castelfranco Emilia is one of many placid, overgrown villages so complacent in their prosperity that they seem unaffected by the main road that starts at Bologna and cuts through the towns one after another as far as Modena, then Reggio, Parma and beyond. There is not a great deal to do in Castelfranco Emilia except work or wait for the commuters to come home in the evening.

Then Saturday arrives and all of them, from the grandparents down, go off to the supermarket on a shopping spree. The town lives immersed in a culture that respects *doing* above all things, its down-to-earth inhabitants convinced that work is the only thing worth living for. They no longer notice the arterial road, packed with trucks and the station-wagons of commercial travellers, that splits the town in half like a blow from a cleaver. Here a child is free to choose whether to breathe fog or foul air, to live in exhaust fumes or the stench of the excrement of the thousands of pigs surrounding the town. Here one soon learns that life is dangerous and poisonous, like a big car, like pork fat.

In Castelfranco Emilia the posters for the local papers hardly ever announce anything exciting. Sometimes they highlight the death of a pensioner crushed by a truck, at other times the umpteenth project for a bypass to free the helpless citizens from smog and the stink of hot tyres; or else, on a really good day, the elopement of a local businessman with his young secretary.

And yet for a few days Castelfranco Emilia magnetised the attention of the national press; the television news actually mentioned the name of the place. At the centre of this unhoped-for slice of provincial life, was a highly successful film, *Titanic*, its star, Leonardo Di Caprio, the idol of teenage girls half the world over, and Marika, one of the many fans besotted with Leonardo's pretty face and the story of love and death consummated on the deck of that ill-fated liner. The fact is that Marika has seen this film more than fifty times running, every day since it began showing in the town cinema. In Castelfranco Emilia there is only one cinema, and every afternoon she waits for the doors to open to see her *Titanic* again. Of course one can understand that the distributors are only too pleased to season the already extraordinary success of the film with the sugary tones of a little village fairy-tale; rather less understandable is the interest of the press, the interviews with the young fan, her parents, the owner of the cinema who generously reserves a seat for the girl every afternoon. Mention is even made of a request by some fellow citizen that this new candidate for the Guinness Book of Records should be adequately rewarded by the film's producers, perhaps with a medal or a signed photograph of the handsome Di Caprio.

But this journalistic tittle-tattle does not mention anyone who wonders why, every afternoon, Marika feels the irrepressible urge to go and see *Titanic*. A crush on the mythical Leonardo is not sufficient explanation; perhaps there is more to it, something to do not only with Marika's condition of being in love with a film star, but also with the situation of many of her contemporaries.

Should we not be worried about Marika's loneliness? Should we not to want to look into the causes of this existential void, and its lack of adult reference points? What is there for a young girl to do at five in the afternoon in Castelfranco Emilia or any other town in

Italy? Maybe, instead of daydreaming about Leonardo Di Caprio, she should endure hours and hours of fatuous television chat-shows, or drag herself to a gym or the nearest bar, if only to meet someone else.

Other than money, what do the young of those prosperous Po Valley regions get from their parents, people who work unceasingly from dawn till dusk, accumulating riches they never have time to enjoy? Ultimately, who is in a position to show these adolescents a little affection? The swimming-pool attendant? The owner of the amusement arcade? Leonardo Di Caprio? What is provided for these teenagers by the much-vaunted 'good government' of those regions, of those cities?

And now that *Titanic* has finished its run, what will become of Marika?

Adolescence and identity

Creatures of the night

Video images flicker on the lunar landscapes of their rooms; earphones are at full volume; computers navigate the globe. It is night; the time they like best. The time to take the car or the moped and tour the town, deserted at last. And then on to the bars and discos, which never close. And they, the young of the night, are like so many Mr Hydes, changing with the falling shadows, trying to live in another dimension, one that is barred to adults. Then dawn comes and they have to turn back into Dr Jekylls, do well at school, put up with Mum's grumbles and Dad's silences. They get through the day holding their breath, thinking of the night ahead.

For many of the young today the fascination of the night has increased. This is when they are less under the control of their parents, while daytime probably brings a slight uneasiness, revealing a difficulty in relating to the adult world. They love the night because it is the only time in their lives when adults are absent. Night is a time free of torment, anxiety, demands. When night falls the grown-ups at last fall silent, go to sleep. And the young can breathe. These are the hours when judgement is suspended.

Night is the space in which the emotions and imagination wander most freely, a time which many young people would like to last for ever. At night they can hope not to be recognised, weighed up, analysed. Darkness creates space to explore one's potential, a chance to re-invent oneself. Behind the nocturnal anonymity of casual chat, a freedom which real life denies in the daytime, can be expressed.

Above all, nighttime enables them not to fear invisibility.

In my day we used to love the bars with billiard tables, where we went to play, to talk and to do nothing. If Mario or Giorgio didn't show up for several afternoons running, we went to see them. All of us knew where each other lived, even which bell to press. Therefore we existed.

Today many youngsters spend their afternoons in amusement arcades in which adults have created for them the most absolute kind of technological autism. And if it so happens that Mario or Giorgio don't show up, who notices, who knows where they live and which is their doorbell?

How many of them are afraid of not existing as individuals, of having become mere ectoplasm in a society of exhibitionists? It is a hard thing to be aware of one's own invisibility at an age when one would like to break the world apart, to shout out one's longing to be in it and to be noticed.

Nighttime leads them to an anonymity that they themselves have chosen: no one knows anything about them and they know nothing about others. In this way the game of life is less painful.

But once the darkness has gone they have to invent another day. For many of the young this becomes increasingly difficult.

The adolescent and his double

On a night of dead calm a young captain is at the wheel of his ship, clad only in pyjamas. The crew is sleeping below decks. At a certain point the moonlight falls on the body of a shipwrecked mariner. The young captain looks at him with puzzlement and curiosity. Who is that man in the sea, not shouting for help? Where does he come from, and why those disturbing features?

So begins one of Joseph Conrad's finest short stories, *The Secret Sharer*.

That man is none other than the captain himself, or rather his other self, his mirror-image, his equal and different identity. The fascination of that body, apparently lifeless and extraneous, is therefore something that resembles him, that disturbs and yet belongs to him.

The mirror is the device adolescents use most, as indispensable as it is feared. In that sheet of glass they investigate their own bodies, their transformation, the gradual definition of a potential form. The mirror reflects fears, condenses the dread that accompanies the growth of an identity still contradictory and ambiguous. It is the place and time where the other part of them is revealed, often the most humiliating, sometimes the farthest from the image they would like to build up for themselves. Looking at himself in the mirror, an adolescent unconsciously creates the space of his own double, the image of his own secret, inscrutable complexity.

The mirror, a form of narcisism that we need if we are to continue, without vanity, to seek our true individual identity. As W.B. Yeats wrote:

> *From mirror after mirror*
> *No vanity's displayed*
> *I'm looking for the face I had*
> *Before the world was made.*

It is difficult to be an adolescent today, far more complicated than it was thirty years ago. At one time we were less likely to be judged by our peers, and were chiefly afraid of the moralising of grown-ups. To go to a disco today you have to be immaculate: thin, gym-fit, fashionably dressed, witty, seductive, involved. To achieve success at school you have to be aggressive, competitive, hot on performance, charismatic. The impetus that drives teenagers towards uniformity of lifestyle seems to be increasingly brutal and effective. In order to exist you have to conform to that average model, that shared mediocrity, even at the cost of losing some part of your outward appearance. During a debate in Como a woman once told me that many girls in that city, on reaching their 18th birthday, ask their parents for plastic surgery. And they get it.

Some young people, however, are aware of this danger and struggle to pursue a course of their own, a search that leads them to introspection, and sometimes to a kind of neo-mysticism. Hence the spread of the New Age cultures or the successful proselitising of certain doctrines, even to the point of sectarian fanaticism. In other words a scarch – not always a conscious search – for spirituality runs counter to the banal appeal of material consumerism from which most of the young seem unable to escape.

The fear of diversity

The attention of adolescents is attracted and at the same time repelled by the search for their own double, and the fear that the adults have of diversity are often reflected in them.

I remember that on a visit to Venice a few weeks before he was assassinated, Yitzhak Rabin told a moral fable about the Rialto bridge.

> *It was built precisely between East and West, at a time when those who crossed it eastward were looking for new spaces, new lands, new peoples. Those were the years of the apogee of a civilisation, and its consecration coincided with the need for the Other, with the search for what was new and different. Those who set forth were the boldest, the most independent with regard to their own roots, but the benefit was felt by a whole community, which learned that going towards the unknown might not signify desperation but growth. For a whole people came wealth, scientific*

discoveries, cultural development. But later that same bridge was crossed in the opposite direction, from East to West. Many were those who returned to their own homes, to cultivate their own gardens, within the walls of domestic security. Those were the years of fear of the Other, the age in which diversity ceased to be a resource and became an obscure menace. It was the time of the darkest regression, the eclipse of this same civilisation.

We need only think of the many children born and growing up in the one-family villas of our residential suburbs. Places that ought to represent prosperity and social status have instead become little fortresses in which a family lives behind barricades of suspicion, villas protected by walls, watched day and night by closed-circuit television, with fierce dogs guarding the well kept gardens. How will they be as adults, the children who grow up in such distressing isolation? What will they think of others, of those different from themselves, if as children they have learned to fear and hate them?

Such a paranoid view of existence cannot fail to make social and emotional relationships less common and more superficial, and lead to even greater difficulty in the quest for the other. The range of communication will increasingly tend to shrink, people will turn inwards as if a feeling of extraneousness has in the end succeeded in pervading and annulling what is external to all of us – otherness.

How can we fail to see that the culture of diversity is the only antidote to indifference, which is the worst 'obscure malady' threatening the young generations? Or that the good things that do find expression – good music, good architecture, good art, good cinema, the very essence of the best creativity of man – depend on diversity?

The glorification of egocentricity threatens to lead many of the young to place too much value on their own inner world, including that duality which today, released from simplifying moralistic rules, paradoxically becomes even more disquieting and perturbing for them.

A high percentage of adolescents, turning the search for otherness towards themselves, are induced to discover the perverse fascination of their own innermost duality. They boost it so much as to show it off as an endowment, so that the only diversity acceptable to their culture risks being solely that area of their personality governed by the extraordinary resource of their inner and secret ambiguity.

Here, then, is one of the possible reasons for which so many young people love the most recent forms of virtual communication, for example the 'chatlines' which, while ensuring absolute anonymity, stress the need for anxiety, the search for what has been suppressed, for a diversity not admitted elsewhere. The internet and the new technologies of communication thus threaten to become an anti-conventional convention, the only one through which it is possible to

be accepted as different on condition that, outside that
virtual sphere, they return to being slaves to the most
rigid standardisation – as used to happen in a number of
trendy discos some years ago, or happens in all the
carnivals that ever were.

Look closely – no one is normal

On the flaking plaster of a wall in the Trieste lunatic
asylum, vacated thanks to the self-sacrifice and
creativity of Franco Basaglia, one of the leading lights
of Italian culture, someone wrote in huge letters: 'If you
take a good look, no one is normal.'

The great fear which increasingly leads adolescents
to take no interest in others and to concentrate entirely
on themselves does, however, offer us a chance to
understand something more of the cultures and
languages of communication. Theirs is a route which
brings them to a better knowledge of their own inner
life, an understanding of its complexity without
necessarily having recourse to repression or psychological treatment.

How can we say they are wrong, seeing that
psychoanalysts themselves are so frightened by what
they have begun to catch glimpses of as to draw very
pessimistic conclusions about the nature of the psyche:
if man were not equipped with powerful defence
systems he would be prey to destructive and self-
punitive impulses.

But one innovatory, if minority, element in youth culture believes that it is possible to live with one's own duality, maintains that a full account of existence is based also on the acceptance of one's own double, one's own ambivalence.

According to this view, the life of the psyche unfolds in a continuous conflict between the tendency to exorcise evil and the need to encourage what is good. Man is neither one thing nor the other, but a constant intermingling of the two opposites, a symbiosis between attraction and repulsion, the need for enjoyment and the inevitability of suffering, between life and death.

Until not so long ago we had a more limited awareness of this inner tangle, and this enabled us to act without being oppressed by feelings of guilt. Today a number of young people have all too clear a view or intuition of their own inner discord; they accept it as an auspicious, anthropological mutation with respect to the hypocritical conformist mortalising of earlier generations.

Sexual identity

We need only observe the change in the concept of sexual identity in the most recent youth cultures. At one time this identity was firmly established within certain and accepted limits. Any ambivalence presumed a departure from the norm, and therefore led to a painful social exclusion. Today sexual identity no longer follows the pre-established membership of a group. Literature, cinema, advertising, fashion, all these tend to use this transition as a resource: amongst young people the masculinisation of the female and the feminisation of the male provide an interesting aid to understanding a complex process of change.

> *The word 'sexuality' has become laden with too many ambiguities. We no longer know what it means. We seem to have returned to Babel, to the time of the confusion of tongues . . . Perhaps we should therefore cease to speak of sexuality, indeed perhaps we should be even more drastic: abolish the word itself as being old and withered . . . At least until we have become reaccustomed to thinking of sexuality as a human reality it is expedient to go back for a while to the terminology used by God, who does not speak of sexuality but of man and woman.*

Thus declaimed (and the word is all too apt) the editorial of one of the most authoritative Catholic periodicals.

We are struck here by the way 'ambiguity' is given a bad name, as if sexuality was not also twofold. The very fact of not being able to consider it a resource (as in the case of diversity) has turned sexuality into a form of anxiety which many find hard to bear. To speak today of man and woman as two distinct psychological entities is really bizarre. A century of psychoanalysis and decades of feminist thinking have not been enough to dismantle a fanciful notion that was always purely male. At this time, when many of our young people of both sexes are beginning to understand something about it, must we blot out the word sexuality? Now, when our children associate with and learn to know the other sex from nursery school onward, instead of discovering it at the age of 15, must we go back to segregation, to stockades bristling with sex phobias?

What is most frightening to no small section of the adult population, homosexuality, the masculinisation of the female or the feminisation of the male? Are they more upset by the affected pigtails of the young male or the uncouth tattoos of the young female? Could it be that what worries stick-in-the-mud adults is the thought that equal opportunities, which at last have become a reality, have led many young women to think of themselves as more independent?

Never, as they can today, have young women been able to dare to plan motherhood without a partner, to programme it despite biological obstacles which were insuperable until yesterday. Science makes all this possible. The male, pushed ever more to the sidelines, fears that his power will be undermined.

In the streets of every city one sees self-confident and purposeful young girls, while many young boys seem de-structured and full of complexes. Some time ago in a secondary school in Treviso, during an assembly in which we discussed loving and reciprocal love, I heard a boy very bravely and painfully describe his own troubles, his recent failure in love. Only twenty years ago that lad would have been ashamed of such feelings, of not presenting himself in the eyes of his fellows as a macho lady-killer, one who 'never has to ask', the pride and joy of so many parents, a symbolic object for so much trashy advertising.

The emergence of this uncertainty today offers a great opportunity; a woman who grows up stronger and more resolute will certainly gain more respect than her mother did, while a more sensitive boy will become less superficial and indifferent to the emotions than his father was.

Ultimately the word sexuality means above all 'relationship'. In an age of frigid emotional relationships I really do not think that 'sexuality' should be the first word to be amended. Instead it would be interesting to ask ourselves what role the schools and other educational agencies might play with regard to the culture of sexuality.

Though there is more awareness of it, if you listen to them carefully, still dormant in many youngsters is the need for an *'éducation sentimentale'*. Not courses in 'sexual education', which are useless, but guided tours, situations in which (responsible and enthusiastic) adult men and women are capable of educating girls and boys about the importance of relationships.

Seeking independence

Autonomy is strength

Supper with friends here in Italy on the occasion of the visit of a colleague of mine from Denmark. After the meal we are chatting in the sitting-room when the daughter of our hosts comes in, a handsome young woman of thirtyish who joins in our conversation. My Danish colleague, his tongue perhaps loosened by wine, asks her how on earth she happens to be there with her parents; whereupon they, their pride offended, declare that their daughter has never left the family. But the Dane's astonishment turns to bewilderment when he learns that not only is this young woman quite content with her dependent status, but the parents are even happier about it than she is. I do my best to explain to him that this is not a freak family, but faithfully reflects much of the situation as it exists throughout Italy: seven youngsters out of ten decide to go on living with Mum even after the age of 35, and over half of the single parents prefer to stay in the same block of flats as their family.

My Danish colleague is dumbfounded and asks if this phenomenon looms large in my clinical practice. I answer by describing a scene that occurs regularly in my consulting room.

The protagonists are a father, mother and son or daughter slightly over 20 years old. The parents are usually well-off.

The son (or daughter) is studying at the university but does not sit the exams; in fact he or she does next to nothing except 'attend', which means leaving the house in the evening, shifting from one bar to another, from a pizzeria to a friend's house, from some piazza to a disco, and so on until dawn. They drink and talk a lot, they take some drugs but only on Saturdays.

According to the scenario the mother asks her son/daughter why he/she doesn't study harder, and the reply is: 'I don't like it and I'll do it when and if I want to.' At this point the father asks why they don't look for a job, and the son/daughter replies that there aren't any jobs going, let alone the one they want (but are unable to describe). The father thereupon says: 'But you can't stay here doing nothing, why don't you leave home?' And the answer is: 'Why should I? I'm comfortable here and rents are too high.'

Such a scene usually continues for a while, until one of the parents asks the ultimate question: 'But what do you want to do in life?' To which the reply is: 'Absolutely nothing. You have three apartments, so there's one for you, one for me, and the other I can rent and live on the money. That would do me fine.'

These are not isolated cases; they are part of what one sociologist optimistically called 'protracted adolescence', meaning that typically Italian phenomenon whereby the young of both sexes live in their parents' home as if it were a hotel. They are always there, lunch and dinner, they bring their partners to sleep in their bedrooms, and sometimes even demand an allowance just as they did when they were 15.

Certainly there is no lack of 'external' motives or

justification. There really is a shortage of jobs, and as for reasonable rents, forget it. After all, they are really very comfortable at home, there is less conflict and more freedom than there used to be, so the reasons for leaving grow weaker and weaker and the temptation to stay becomes irresistible. What's more, all things considered, it is not displeasing to the parents that their role is still so important to their children. It is the confirmation that they still have a little power, that they can go on worrying about them.

For many young people in Italy dependence on their parents is taken for granted and not open to question. They probably think they deserve some kind of compensation from the family for what the State has failed to do for them. In any case, to be maintained by one's parents has become a right which the Court recently embodied in a sentence. Are the young therefore right in demanding, and the parents right in doling out, financial aid until an age at which one time would have been considered that of full maturity and independence?

No national or local administration has ever produced a housing plan to address this problem. On the few occasions when such a proposal has been put forward, everything has boiled down to a loan on easy terms restricted to young couples or those just about to get married. According to our government, therefore, the young are all right living in the old homestead. If any of them really need to be helped, it is only those who decide to get married who are entitled to any assistance; as if, at that age, some experience of informal cohabitation was not essential.

The scant attention paid to the conditions necessary for learning how to be independent conceals the obvious discomfort with which adults face the approaching maturity of their children. The request to be allowed to leave home is widely read as a form of rejection and ingratitude towards those who 'have done so much for them'.

But leaving the parental home at the end of adolescence is an obligatory and essential part of growing up. It does not mean betraying the affection of Mum and Dad. On the contrary, it enables one to understand the strength of this bond from outside, without being forced to live together. It was not for nothing that the English invented the boarding school, to create an intermediate zone between dependence on the family and independent life, able to protect the adolescent for a number of years while obliging him also to measure up to the earliest responsibilities of adult life. Not having a resource such as boarding schools, we might at least encourage young people who wish to continue their studies after school-leaving certificate to attend a university in another town.

This choice would compel them to face different and new styles of living. Having a living-space of one's own means being in control of one's day-to-day existence, testing one's ability to organise one's life, exposing oneself to the possibility of experiencing emotions and affections outside the control of adults. In order to experience all that, it is essential to live some period of one's life without having to set up a new family unit of one's own.

If more parents had the courage to do this, they could help their children to grow up more mature, less fragile, and therefore less open to emotional blackmail.

The dependence of the young on their parents is not due solely to economic circumstances. Talking recently with a group of 30-year-olds in the province of Udine, I realised that most of them, although they had well-paid jobs, and were therefore able to rent a flat and live independently, by no means considered leaving their parents an absolutely necessary step at their age. The question is evidently not an easy one.

For a long time now relations between parents and children have not been such a battlefield. In fact many families pride themselves on the atmosphere of tacit reciprocal understanding they create. Since early adolescence the children have been able to enjoy almost unlimited freedom.

But there is another feature that has altered the picture even more radically, and that is the guilt parents feel about how they have brought their children up. During the evolutionary years attachment and detachment are both determining factors.

From his time in the womb the individual develops towards his mother a deep-seated, obstinate need for dependence, not only from the biological (e.g. nutritional), but also emotional and relational point of view. Ultrasound scans show us that when a mother-to-be strokes her belly, the foetus swims towards the touch of that hand and he begins kicking when his mother stops stroking. This attachment continues long after birth, by way of breast-feeding, the first spoken words, learning to walk. All too often our decisions and sometimes offhand interpretation of our rights as adults have weakened this phase of growth. Breast-feeding stops earlier, the child is separated sooner from its mother, surrogate figures such as baby-sitters and day-nursery staff loom larger. The awareness that such a profound change in the earliest phase of growth is not always altogether necessary or advantageous for a child leads to a deep, agonising sense of guilt in many parents, which in turn induces them to try to make up for it. Such parents become less assertive, have recourse to presents and money as a form of compensation for their absence, depart more easily from the rules and timetables of domestic life.

When the time approaches to move out, that is the age at which the adolescent has to begin to test his own capacity for independence; the need to make amends prompted by guilt feelings leads to the endless delaying of the various stages of loosening the emotional ties. It is the parents themselves who do not feel ready to encourage the necessary separation. The relationship between parents and children thus takes on the characteristics of a contest between adolescents, two immature parties, mediated by reciprocal emotional blackmail.

Teaching an adolescent how to make a gradual

progress towards independence is of fundamental importance. Many years ago, whenever possible, I would meet Cesare Musatti, pioneer of Italian psychoanalysis. He was already an old man at that time and I was a young idealistic psychiatrist who thought it proper to aspire to 'cure' patients rather than help them to understand and consciously, independently, accept their own diversity. I remember that one evening I asked him: 'How does one know when a person is better, when he's on the road to recovery?' And he, stroking his long white hair, with an ironic smile replied: 'When he stops sending you Christmas cards.'

This lesson in life certainly doesn't apply only to a psychotherapist but to every adult, because we are all educators. To love someone means to see them grow, to love their dependence is just sheer egoism.

The processes that make us independent are therefore inevitably connected with severing our earliest bonds of love. Maturity is responsibility, and responsibility is not misfortune (which it is often made out to be by adults) but freedom. The time of least responsibility coincides with the period of our lives – infancy – when we are least free, the time when we are most in control is the one which brings with it the full acceptance of our social and family responsibilities.

Teaching independence means teaching how to live life. One day a young man said to me: 'My dad has always filled up my moped for me. Now that I'm grown up I don't even know where the petrol pump is.'

The family and decline

'Respectable' families

Two half-naked teenagers sitting on a bed, a kiss that seems to last for ever, shot in the most minute detail, no soundtrack except for their gasps, not even a whispered word. This is the opening of one of the most disquieting films of recent years, *Kids*. Along with the much more famous winner of many Oscars, *American Beauty*, it bears embarrassing, tough and terribly important witness to the situation of young people today.

Only just over forty years ago our parents were upset by *Rebel Without a Cause*, a prophetic film about the 'Lost Generation' and its heroes, all of whom perished in dramatic circumstances, including James Dean, Natalie Wood and the legendary director Nicholas Ray.

Today these two films cast a fierce and pitiless look at our children – and their parents. The reaction of the stick-in-the-muds to both films was to be absolutely furious. There were those who accused *Kids* of nihilistic paedophilia, others who hoped that no adolescent would ever go and see *American Beauty*. In a more charitable spirit, a few people considered these films to be an alarm bell for families, a warning of the dangers that children and adolescents are exposed to when they are neglected.

The interest of these two films is by no means purely cinematographic. Their chief merit resides not only in having the courage to portray the everyday life of a teenage girl and her circle with great fidelity: days spent between sex, tedious gatherings with friends to watch filmstrips of skateboard riding, smoking pot or planning to hunt down the local virgins or playing at seducing some of Dad's 50-year-old friends. And then petty theft at the supermarket or out of their parents' pockets, discos bursting with hallucinatory drugs, punitive expeditions against some poor tramp, orgiastic parties. Or again, love-yearnings at long distance, tedious classrooms, the usual dull little parties.

The contribution made by these two films resides chiefly in their having portrayed our 'respectable' families, and the absence of adults, without moralising or sugaring the pill; showing us a pathetic mother suckling her new baby while smoking and watching a soap opera, or another neurotically pursuing her career; and fathers without individuality, intent only on not growing old.

This is why these films caused so much apprehension in our media: they did not depict extraordinary or marginal cases but, with a large dose of irony, showed us our own neighbourhoods, our domestic lives, the everyday occurrences which are in some measure part of each one of us.

Andria, a large urban area north of Bari: four teenage sons of prominent local families decoy a little girl, attempt to abuse her sexually, burn her alive. Treviso: the police arrest three scions of leading families who were peddling drugs in the discos and only a few days later a girl hammers her ex-fiancé to death for the sake

132

of a couple of happy pills. Varese: well-off youngsters murder a prostitute. Chiavenna, near Sondrio: three secondary schoolboys knife an elderly nun to death.

Which scares us most, the reality or the celluloid fiction? Are we more upset by scenes in a film or by the reports in our newspapers?

For many adults trying to understand adolescence means being afraid of it. The young protagonists of those films live too close to us, are tremendously like our children or those of the family next door. Grown-ups sense that this state of affairs is not a Hollywood invention but is cruelly close to our own everyday reality. A neighbourhood in New York is not all that unlike Andria or Varese, the boredom and indifference depicted in those films are not so different from those experienced by juvenile murderers in our own cities. The homes in which emotions have evaporated, where the absent parents are capable of mutual hatred without leaving each other, where the schools exert no influence for the better: are such things mere Hollywood exaggerations? Do we really not see that same despairing resignation emerge from reports of what happens in our own cities?

The media ritually inform us of often horrendous crimes committed by adolescents, and go on to say that the latter are children of 'respectable families'. In the most serious cases the article also includes comments by neighbours, acquaintances and relatives who in unison repeat the phrase: 'They were good lads . . . I would never have expected it . . .' If the truth be told many adults in our community no longer know what to expect.

Who are these so-called respectable families? Personally I have never understood the term, and I fear that respectable journalists mean those of professional men, the rich who live in the posh neighbourhoods and go about town in expensive cars. From these privileged families, applying a strange form of social positivism, we expect every kind of 'good', simply because they have bought the appearances. According to this convenient simplification, social well-being cannot produce any kind of ill-being. It all takes on the shape of a huge collective act of self-acquittal, and cheap at the price.

For decades we have seen the most extreme forms of psychological malfunctioning correlated with conditions of social and economic inferiority. This brought about a promising view of the future: our community could nourish the hope that with progress and a better distribution of resources certain forms of psychological suffering would be reduced. This has not come to pass: not only does social exclusion still produce devastating damage to individuals, but a new and unexpected factor has entered the lists: the disease of prosperity itself. And the worst of it is that the forms of ill-being induced by economic well-being call for much more complex solutions. Charity is not enough.

Gorilla cubs

Further signs of the progressive decline of our little western world:

A sultry afternoon. A hypermarket on the outskirts of a big city. The man in front of me in the queue for the cash desk has a trolley full of video game cassettes. The cashier quickly taps out the prices, then suddenly slows down, picks up one cassette and scrutinises it, reads out the name, wrinkles her brow as if to show her disapproval of that purchase, then sternly asks: 'Have you got adolescent children? I should warn you that this video game is for adults only'. The game is called 'Carmageddon 2', the latest, most cynical and cruel of the violent video games that have long since flooded a market that has no ethical rules whatever. On the surface it is only a car race with a track providing a series of driving hazards. Except that the scoring is not based on the skill and experience of the driver but on his basest instinct; for the points are awarded according to the number of people (mostly unknowing pedestrians, mothers on the way home with their shopping bags, tottering old women) who are hit, run over and crushed by the car which the player is 'driving'. Needless to say, 'Carmageddon 2' sold like hot cakes.

One summer night in Turin a group of youngsters celebrates passing the school-leaving certificate. They are nearly all drunk, and the only place still open is a bar down by the river – by no means the quietest part of the city, especially at that hour. There are drug pushers, prostitutes, tramps sleeping on sheets of cardboard. Our group comes across a young black man, maybe a pusher or maybe just a foreigner who has lost his way. A quarrel breaks out, with yelling and punching, and finally a powerful shove. The black man falls or is pushed into the water. The lads laugh at his clumsiness as he struggles and calls for help, while for their part they throw a fruit-box at his head. It all happens in a moment, yet it seems like a film played in slow motion. They go on laughing as the victim's gestures grow ever more frantic. A minute or two later he moves no more. He is drowned.

Who are these young people, capable of playing at death in a video game but also in reality, of killing housewives in 'Carmageddon 2' and repeating their exploits with a dark-skinned contemporary on the banks of the Po? What if film director Oliver Stone were right when in his *Natural Born Killers* he has a character say: 'Those boys know the difference between right and wrong, and they don't care'? What if Falco Blask were right in describing those youngsters as part of the Q generation (which takes its name from one of the the characters in *Star Trek*)? Young people without scruples, amoral, egocentric, hedonistic, danger-loving, guided by an idea of omnipotence, unpredictable, calculating that wrong-doing is the only way to achieve success, absolutely convinced that they no longer have anything to lose . . .

Some may think this simply the most recent of many

sociological classifications, others a zany splinter group, the tiny exception that proves the goodness of most of today's young people. But what if the Q generation appeared ever more disconcertingly to be the demonstration of how much some of our young resemble the worst part of the adult world? Would it not then be permissible to ask from whom they have learned such harmful lessons? But before we are baffled by their most tragic rituals, before we pronounce our (I hope) rightful and inflexible judgement on their responsibilities, should we not concern ourselves with those who have set them such a bad example?

What can lead these 'gorilla cubs' to commit such acts: desperation, boredom, genetic predisposition, perverse impulses, social or family influences? We need to ask ourselves how they live as young gorillas, what reality *is* when seen through their eyes. Let me make it clear that I do not use the phrase 'gorilla cubs' to evoke any feelings of sympathy towards a delinquent who has killed in cold blood. Just as young people have a right to their individuality, they also have responsibilities, and must learn to fulfil them. Society must be very rigorous towards those who have dared failed to do so.

The problem is that the grown-ups always arrive late. They do not know how to predict events but only how to describe them, and they frequently act after the event itself has occurred; the facts are never interpreted according to their causes but only by their superficial manifestations. A century of psychoanalysis has not helped us to distinguish our culture from that of the entomologist, who only has to stick a pin through the insect he wishes to classify.

If many youths resemble young gorillas, the problem lies not with the young but with the gorillas who gave birth to them.

As long as we continue to think of a young murderer simply as the product of a degraded environment, we will be fostering a prejudice that leads to absolute pessimism, a surrender on behalf of the destinies of a whole community. If, on the other hand, there really were such a thing as *raptus* or irrational impulse, perhaps genetically passed on, it would mean that human actions are dictated purely by impulse; there would be no learning, no relationships, no emotional sympathy, but only instinctive reaction without responsible thought. But if this were really the case, if man were prey to unintelligible impulses, aggressive towards himself and others, our species would not have had the least chance of survival.

Such rooted prejudices perform certain useful functions when it comes to safeguarding our consciences. If a youngster is marked down as a monster, because he is a social freak or the product of some perverse genetic joke, then all the other lads are virtuous and biologically sound. We need only persecute and punish those few for all the others – our own children – to be safe. On the other hand, such genetic and biological causal hypotheses are extremely reassuring, in that they eliminate at source all responsibilities, both individual and collective.

If, however, we think that something in the mechanism that led that murderer to kill is shared by many other youths of his age, then our consciences are far from being unscathed. Events often become mirrors. We need only take a careful look at the histories of so many delinquent youngsters to distinguish a number of elements they have in common with others who do not kill or commit crimes: lack of affection, indifference, an emotional void . . .

Alberto Arbasino has written:

> *The luckless histories of the Italian 'lost' (and now aging) generation leave us distressed and disappointed because from so many years of confused agitation nothing beneficial for the country ever seems to emerge . . . The taste for everything that proves to be parasitic or destructive in the community leads in the end to depression or anorexia, because it is not the result of strong ideals, grand projects, dramatic personalities, but only a by-product of superficiality, indifference, opportunism and bungling.*

There is often a tendency to drag in the decline in values or the damaging role of television as factors in the increase in juvenile crime. There are those who pompously declare that we live in a society without morality or ethics; there is talk of money, the craving for excess, the cynical and egotistical relationships between individuals. However, in all honesty, we should add that money, aggression and the cult of excess are never represented as negative values but, on the contrary, as what the majority of people ought to aspire to, to the extent of wanting to teach them to their children.

This is how the young gorillas grow up. Are television and magazines not positively oozing with this culture? Are the heroes of today mild, sober, modest men and women? Is there a contemporary example which the young can dream of and imitate that has not been constructed according to the rules of ostentation, aggression and the last degree of narcissism?

Some months ago a well-known psychoanalyst took me to task in the columns of a newspaper because I had stated that, 'every society, like every individual, has the children it deserves'. Perhaps my esteemed colleague had something on his conscience that he didn't manage to forgive himself for. However, not a day passes without my becoming increasingly sure of the truth of those words. And I do not mean this as a sort of biblical anathema, but as the best and most felicitous challenge that a community and an individual can take up: the aspiration of a group, of a parent, of an educator, to create conditions for the greater happiness of future generations. So that what they inherit is not only our faults and our guilt.

We would need to start from the beginning, by listening to children and adolescents. Can we do it? Are we willing to?

The time for listening

With the boys and girls of a secondary school in Genoa I once played at 'time'. The rules are simple. You divide the class into two or three groups and each one has to analyse a certain part of any day, minute by minute. Some of the things that emerged were predictable, others less so. For example, I did not know how long it takes, on average, for a girl to remove her make-up in the evening: about eleven minutes. It is one of the most self-centred operations that an adolescent can perform; there is no one with her and she has to use both hands, so she is unable even to chat with a friend on the telephone or send messages.

The most surprising thing is that this period of solitude is almost exactly the same as the time spent on family life, i.e., supper. The average time spent at table for the evening meal is thirteen minutes in all, including the television news. Once it is over the family splits up in a sort of diaspora: Dad stretches out on the sitting-room sofa to watch television, Mum goes into the kitchen to finish the chores, the adolescent shuts herself up in her technological tomb to play with her playstation, to telephone and chat with her friends. If you want to scare an adolescent to death try suggesting spending twenty-six minutes over supper. He or she would be horrified.

What, then, can one talk about in the thirteen minutes at table with Mum and Dad? Both language and its contents must conform to the time available.

One will therefore choose to talk about money and school, the subjects at the top of the list, and avoid tackling emotional questions, which would take too much time and in fact come last of all the matters discussed. The parents' questions tend to be as repetitious as a litany at evensong, with the replies being just as conclusive: 'How did it go at school?' 'Not bad'. Full stop. End of the evening's conversation.

It is therefore clear that, if this is the daily ration of communication in many Italian families, it becomes difficult to foresee, to feel and to intervene when the life-problems of adolescents get in too much of a tangle when they are growing up.

Talking about feelings and emotions not only answers the expectations of our young, but it lets the adult know about the state of mind in that evolving life, its ability to face up to untoward events, the extent of its self-respect.

A recent survey of a representative sample of Italian adolescents tells us that 60% of them have a computer, playstation and mobile phone in their bedrooms. This means on the one hand that the adults wish to segregate them, to isolate them in a little privileged ghetto where they are allowed to do whatever they want, and on the other that the young people themselves do not seek contact with their families.

Our community is building up a kind of reciprocal autism, with parents and children who don't know each other, living together on a merely superficial and conventional level. All this to persuade us that they are good respectable families.

A noisy silence

They call themselves squatters. They are very colourful and frightening. Some time ago they literally beseiged Turin. The surrender of this city to the demands of industry was forced to come to terms with the explosion of a small movement of lawless youngsters without roots. People bolted their doors, the shops pulled down their shutters, scared by the violence of that eccentric horde. And the squatters, gathering together to commemorate one of their number who had committed suicide in jail, proclaimed their hatred of everything and everyone, leaving no doubt about their own alienation. For hours and for days the panic spread amongst inhabitants and journalists alike. Everybody suddenly discovered that they were weak and defenceless.

The philosopher Gianni Vattimo wrote in a Turinese newspaper of the squatters, that apart from the fear they induced, there was nothing to be understood. He maintained that behind their anarchic slogans there were no ideas; the few they proclaimed were part of a heritage by no means peculiar to them. According to Vattimo, the squatters represented nothing new, only the repetition of an old form of vacuous and tritely nihilistic extremism.

Behind the dyed hair, the most improbable body-piercings and the enormous ambiguities there lies a metaphor that is useful even to our adult world. The question is not what that horde of hooligans should have communicated, but the fact that they did not want to communicate anything. The novelty this time is to be found in their stubborn silence.

That silence not only demonstrated the utter denial by a minority of all that surrounds it and from which it is excluded; on the contrary it is the exemplification – hence the metaphorical aspect – of a situation common to very many others who by no means identify themselves with that bizarre bunch of latter-day anarchists.

Among young people there have always been extremist fringes who have found their own identity in a radical opposition to the system produced by their parents' generation. Although using forms of gratuitous violence, their exploits were accompanied by criticism and even sarcasm. This established at least an attempt at communication, perhaps embittered in manner and argumentative in content, but nonetheless a confrontation between cultures, modes of being, points of view about the world. Even at times of the bitterest contention the clash between generations has included words, the quest for communication. Until now.

The squatters with their stubborn silence mark the end of the last vestige of communication. A disquieting, but not surprising, ending. The roots of this friction lie deep in the economic boom of the 1960s, when the frenetic pace of consumerism that accompanied the economic and technological growth of the western world helped to widen the communication gap between those who proudly encouraged that process of modernisation (the parents' generation) and those who objected to the social inequalities produced by it (the younger generation).

Hence the tendency not only of many of the young, but also persons of sensitivity such as a number of great artists, to dissent, to declare their own difference. We need only call to mind the sequence in one of Michelangelo Antonioni's great films, *Blow-up*, in which four young men 'play tennis' in a London park, moving about on a rectangle of grass as if it were a real tennis court. They play as if they had rackets instead of just hands, they follow the flight of the ball as it crosses the net, but there is no ball and no net either. All this without a word spoken, in a silence broken only by the rustling of leaves.

That prophetic scene – like many of the slogans shouted during those years – was a danger signal: continuing the way that it was going, western society would ruthlessly sacrifice solidarity for egoism, and barter away happiness for opportunism. Today, thirty years after that fantasy game of tennis, some of our young have ceased to talk. Maybe because they are sated with it, or else they are hardened and cynical; maybe because they have been prematurely deprived of hopes and dreams. Not all of them have dyed hair or tattoos, and yet they have no further wish to speak.

The silence of the squatters in Turin is certainly the noisiest one, but equally certainly not the most disquieting.

Our culture of drugs

A drugged community

I well remember that summer of thirty years ago. I was an intern at the Clinic for Nervous Diseases at Verona University. The director, Professor Hrayr Terzian, a man of outstanding culture, intuition and ability to see the problems of the young, had asked us young 'errand-boys' to find out what was going on in a piazza in the centre of town. Circulating there for some weeks past had been a certain white powder, plentiful and free, which had taken the place of the 'soft' drugs. Towards evening the pushers, positioned like crows at the corners of the piazza, were waiting to distribute death to the young people of the city. I was among them, I looked into their faces. They were all more or less my own age, they could have been my friends, they were like me.

Since then more than thirty thousand people in Italy have died from heroin. It has been our Vietnam. If we had buried all those boys and girls together there would have been, in some part of the country, the same vast expanse of identical white crosses as in a war cemetery. Perhaps it would have served to keep alive our memory of an appalling tragedy; it would have taught something to subsequent generations.

We did not do that, we did not want to understand what was happening. Those dead youngsters have been removed wholesale from our consciences. Now people scarcely speak of drugs simply because there are fewer deaths. This has happened due not to the intervention of some ministry, but to the arrival of a threat even greater than that of heroin; a virus and an epidemic that has convinced thousands of addicts to give up using contaminated syringes, and sniff their drug or discover new ones.

And so drugs, and drug-culture, live on among our children.

Heroin has struck down the weakest and most disturbed subjects in entire generations; it has brought out individual and family conflicts, and social and economic contradictions faced with which our community has shown itself even more feeble than those it should have helped and defended. Intervention has been tardy and disorganised. Alongside a very skimpy network of underequipped and understaffed public services, a plethora of communities offering the most diverse and contradictory services has grown up, in an attempt to help thousands of desperate cases and free their families from the neglect in which the State has abandoned them.

People's consciences were not disturbed, so much as their wallets. Heroin addicts stole money and valuables from their homes, stereo radios from their cars, they mugged pensioners and plundered shops. Heroin was regarded chiefly as a social and economic problem. Who those boys or girls actually were, what they were searching for, what had made that enormous chasm in their existence, was not considered that important. Society chose to give precedence to keeping the peace rather than understanding such widespread suffering.

The general cry of 'Do anything as long as you do something' expressed not only a very justified cry of pain and call for help, but also the need to suppress the evidence of one of the most glaring defeats that the process of our social development has ever known. At the beginning many thought that the phenomenon would remain confined to a few urban slums, restricted to complete social dropouts. With the passing of the years, it has become obvious to all that there has been no town so small, no social class so prosperous, that heroin has not overwhelmed it, bringing tears in its wake.

In the public mind all this has tended to reinforce the image of heroin as a catastrophe of biblical proportions, inexorable and of inexplicable origin. Perhaps this is why, when intervention in favour of drug addicts has been discussed, the trend has been to nourish utopian expectations: not treatment but a total cure, not assistance but complete deliverance from the evil. This has led to a situation in which anyone can intervene in this field using any method, without having to show any scientific grounds for what they are doing: from expert psychotherapists to communities where they breed horses, drug addiction has become a no man's land – or rather, everyone's. Anyone in this country has been free to act, any method has been thought permissible, so long as it removes and isolates those who disturb our social serenity and well-being.

Thousands of drug addicts have been employed – and many still are – as an unpaid labour force, under the guise of treatment and rehabilitation. For thirty years dozens of therapeutic communities have in practice made use of a slogan which we cannot speak aloud because of its association with Nazism: *'Arbeit macht frei'*. No one has ever intervened to defend thousands of young people from exploitation carried out in the name of social supervision, treatment, cure. No politician, no trade unionist, no priest (indeed some of these have been and are part of the army of exploiters), and no journalist has had the courage to denounce this scandal. For many years silence has reigned behind those gates, and our consciences have averted their gaze.

And now that heroin no longer bewitches the young as it once did, we turn a blind eye to the mass of cocaine circulating among them. We try to ignore the fact that every year they consume almost a hundred million Ecstasy pills. We only speak of the new drugs if a young man dies in the parking lot of a disco. In the family it is no longer mentioned, nor is it at school. Yet a grasp of the different culture which leads to the use of the drugs would provide us with precious data for the understanding of today's young people, and above all of the changes and the differences between them and the generations before them.

Accepted and unaccepted drug use

Heroin was (perhaps unconsciously) used as an anaesthetic to alleviate the pain of an epoch-making defeat: the defeat of those who in the late 1960s wanted to change the world and failed to do so. It was the drug of individual and group dissent. The heroin addict was a complete outsider, outside society and its rites, its values, and its process of modernisation. His contempt for that world of 'winners' was manifested in the violence with which the drug addict slammed the door in its face, a tremendous rage that often ended in death.

In terms of culture and communication, Ecstasy represents the exact opposite of heroin. Synthetic drugs are not taken to withdraw from other people, but to be accepted by them. Drugs are no longer a megaphone through which to declaim one's own difference, but the means of rejecting all aspirations to social change. The young of today trying out the new drugs seem to be saying: 'The world is all right as it is, all we want is to be part of it.' If heroin was the dramatic cry of those who dreamt of a different world, Ecstasy appears to represent the newest generation's fear of not being accepted by the rules which bind the most consumerist and competitive culture. When I ask a youngster why he takes Ecstasy on Saturday evenings, he replies: 'Because it makes me feel more empathetic'. More approved, accepted, camouflaged.

The consumption of Ecstasy could be interpreted as the antidote to the depressed daily lives of some of the young generation. It reveals uncertainty, the feeling that no one cares, the fear of not mattering enough. Synthetic drugs are an external prop that comes to the aid of a life experience of inadequacy, low self-esteem.

From this point of view the culture surrounding these new drugs bears a close resemblance to that of many adults, many of the parents. How many men and women get up in the morning with Prozac, go to bed with Valium, make love with Viagra? If many adults admit that they have to take chemicals to survive, why on earth should their sons and daughters not do the same?

Having exorcised the social danger of drugs, their impact in terms of money and law and order, and with the large drop in the death rate, our community is in the embarrassing position of having to cope with what it has already largely accepted, and which is part of its own culture.

The new drug addictions therefore metaphorically represent the most obvious contradictions of the world of adults, the inability to provide consistent models, or to be authoritative guides.

With what degree of credibility can we combat an aspect of the world of the young which is so similar to that of adults, and is displayed to our children as an acceptable value for their existence? How are we to oppose alcoholism among the young when it is legal to advertise liquor on television? Why should we be worried about the growing consumption of cigarettes among adolescents when it is the Italian State itself that manufactures and sells them? How can we be concerned about the Saturday night deaths when the leading car manufacturers get Formula One drivers to advertise the models they produce for young people to drive?

Conclusion

It is hard to admit that for the first time in decades the world of the parents so profoundly resembles that of their children; and it is still more embarrassing to admit that the very things which for years have provided necessary grounds for confrontation, and a clear-cut distance between generations, are today the basis for uniformity, making many young people abandon any hopes or plans to make a better world.